To Scottie Webster
who is His and mine
too.

Refocusing God-the Bible and the Church

By

M. F. COTTRELL

DEDICATION

To Kate, and our Wayne, Kent
and Jill; and in memory of my
mother and father who await my
coming.

ACKNOWLEDGEMENTS

For the use of THE BIBLE: A NEW TRANSLATION copyright by James Moffatt, 1954 and used by permission of Harper and Brothers. A translation the author feels to be both meaningful and refreshing in Bible expression for daily living.

For the right to quote from LOVE OR PERISH (C) 1955, 1956, 1957 by Smiley Blanton. Reprinted by permission of Simon and Schuster, Inc. A book we have often recommended for more self-insight and maturity.

We express our eternal gratitude to Cloyd Anthony, Ph. D., Floyd B. Coleman, M.D., and Henry G. Coleman, M.D., who have taught, loved and understood. Perhaps no other person has influenced my life for good and better concepts of New Testament Christianity as has Cloyd Anthony. At the same time, my association and work with the above physicians served to bring me into a closer rapport with The Great Physician and His moving compassion for the human family. Their help to the writer in so many ways can never be returned unless it be in this manner, yet we highly suspect that our mentioning these three men is embarrassingly more than they would prefer. May we also add that we do not wish to leave the impression that they necessarily agree with all we have written. We lay *full* claim only to their love, fellowship and understanding.

7

We wish also to express our thanks to Mrs. Barbara Dalberg, Mrs. Lois Sellars and Mrs. Pat Dalberg for typing the original manuscript. I am indebted to Mrs. Lois Sidebottom for the final one. We also thank Jim Williams for the cover design, and my son Kent for a special and unselfish interest in the general design and appearance of the finished product.

The Author

FOREWORD

PURPOSE

The concepts herein presented have resulted from a restudy of the Bible during the past several years in which we specifically approached the New Testament as the way of life exposed. Our purpose then, is to encourage a sharper look at God, the Bible and the Church—hence our title. We feel the image of all three to be somewhat distorted with consequent loss of original freshness.

GOD

We have attempted to present God as a loving Father, yet as a powerful masculine Friend. Indeed a Friend who is ever interested in us and equal to every situation—One who holds the universe and the times of both men and kingdoms in His hands with certainty!

THE BIBLE

Our look at the Bible is that of a restudy with the aforementioned approach. We attempt to capture some of its freshness, modernity and interest for man in all ages and at the same time point up the sacred volume as one to be diligently studied by the keenest minds for more insight into life and how it ought to operate. As a start in this direction we chose to present several psycho-

9

therapeutic Biblical texts for insight into more abundant living. Not however, as a substitute for dynamic psychiatry (which the Bible can never be) but as correlated material for more emotional insight and self discovery.

THE CHURCH

We have presented rather strong suggestive thought for delivering the church from "churchanity" to the dynamic organism the scriptures seem to indicate. At the same time we have tried to keep our thinking sufficiently balanced so as to permit us to always operate within brotherhood framework. It is our honest opinion that brethren with a *"high blood level of love"* will always tolerate other brethren who attempt to write, providing the writers are equally willing to listen and learn. Finally, it is hoped that we can encourage more capable Christians to think along similar lines and those of us who are less capable to tolerate them while they do it—OUT LOUD!

M. F. C.

TABLE OF CONTENTS

GOD — page 17

Our Spiritual Juvenility
Is God Worried?
Discovery Of God Via Nature
Study of Nature In Youth Camps
Necessity Of "Seeing" God
Results Of "Seeing" Him
Formations Of Concepts — Fear
Love Casteth Out Fear
Hypersensitivity To Scripturalness
    And Its Results
Double Fear — VS — Poise Of Christ
Sinners Cannot Run Away

Chapter 2 — page 32
CHRISTIANS CANNOT RUN AWAY
His Flight (Jonah)
The Storm
Confession And Crises
Reactions
Whoopee! — A Gourd
Lowering The Boom
Summary

Chapter 3 — page 39
THE BIBLE
Re-evaluations
Influencing Factors
Truth Is Fixed But Our Knowledge
    Is Relative
Harm Of Over-Simplification
Some Expressions Of A Slogan

11

TABLE OF CONTENTS

Chapter 4 — page 46

The Lord's Prayer
Kingdom Is More Than "Church Institution"
Kingdom Resources
The Ten Commandments

Chapter 5 — page 51

THE BIBLE AS GOD'S PSYCHOTHERAPY
Learn Of Me
Stupidity Of Sin
Insight Needed
Life Is Relationships
Living Begins With God
Relationships To Others
Handling "Things"
Handling Self
Cheated
Summary

LOVE — As God's Psychotherapy — page 61
We Are Biologically Made To Love
Love Innoculates
It Never Fails
It Never Fails As An Anchor
It Never Fails to Make Peace
Humility
Taking A Sane View
God's Psychotherapy For Worry
An Everyday Example Of Identification And Incorporation
Imagination — vs — The Will
Illness And Suffering

12

TABLE OF CONTENTS

Being Still
Poem: "He Leadeth Me"
Hallelujah! — I Have A Thorn
The Key
The Answer

Chapter 6 — page 89
THE CHURCH
In Relation to God
Fellowship — Its Bigness And Results
Fellowship Is Not To Be Equated
   With 100% Approval
Christ — vs — Phariseeism

WORSHIP
All Facets Of Life Should Express It
City Without A Temple
Worship — Not Confined To A Place
Worship — Not Just Certain "Acts"
Grasping The Dominant Thoughts Of
   Christ
Christ Claimed Divinity Via His
   Program

Chapter 7 — page 103
IDENTIFYING THE CHURCH
Which Group Among Us Is The True
   Church?
"How About This?"
Our Other Brethren
The Real Message Of The So-Called
   Restoration Movement

13

TABLE OF CONTENTS

UNITY

Unity Is Not Uniformity
Patterns And Premises
Patterns
An Analysis

Chapter 8 — page 127
THE LUNENBURG LETTERS
By A. Campbell

Chapter 9 — page 151
COVENANT RELATIONSHIP
Age Factors
Emotional Arrestment
Accountability

Chapter 10 — page 158
CONVERSION
Recognizing Our Two Minds
Cleansing Or Converting The
    Unconscious
Repression
Converting Both Minds
Examples Of Various Reactions
The Thread Of Life
The Disturbance And Re-activation
    Of The Knot Categories
Physical Reactions
How The Knots And Their Re-
    activation Affect Us Religiously
Spiritual Security
The Spiritual Counterpart
Formation Of Spiritual Anchors

TABLE OF CONTENTS

Chapter 11 — page 177
COUNSELLING THE EMOTIONALLY DISTURBED
Introduction
1. Control By Direction
    A Word Of Caution
            ANXIETY
Our Efforts To Avoid It
A Formula
II. Nature Of Anxiety — The Uni-
     versality Of It
     Value Of It
     Our T.R.C.
     Religious Concepts And Anxiety
III. Manifestations
IV. Some Mental Mechanisms
V. Some Sources Of Anxiety
VI. Anxiety Reactions
VII. Phobias
VIII, Depression — A Strong Defense
        Mechanism Against Anxiety
IX. Depression Via Success
X. Obsessions And Compulsions
     (a) Manifestations
     (b) Some Helpful Hints
11. SOME GOALS AND PRIN-
     CIPLES OF GOOD PSYCHO-
     THERAPY
     (a) Improvement of Adaptation
     (b) Self Acceptance
     (c) Internal Improvement
     (d) Reassurance
     Re-evaluation Of Personal Goals
15

Chapter 1

GOD

—Our Spiritual Juvenility—

In an age when man's faith needs to be deepened and God's greatness reappraised, many of us have permitted our faith to remain juvenile and our concepts of God somewhat antiquated. Rather fresh evidence of this is the fact that in these days of space exploration, many sincere souls are exposing their inadequate faith by such remarks as 'Why don't they let space alone and stop tinkering with God's plans." Perhaps those who are so fearful regarding outer space have never really grappled with their own inner space. Juvenile faith is always afraid of test or exposure, and unconsciously this is what many people today are afraid of. Some of us never outgrow our spiritual rompers and any threat to our concepts is almost equated with catastrophe. Such concepts prevent our distinguishing the tornadoes from the ordinary winds and procedures of life.

—Is God Worried?—

Now imagine if you can, a God who is big enough to create the universe and perfectly balance its components and then harmonize that with the likelihood of His being afraid that man will in some way upset that balance. Just here we have in mind church people who pretend to believe in an omnipotent God and by both sermon and song verbalize His greatness; and then by their unconscious leaks tell the whole wide world, "Go easy, it could turn out that God just might not be equal to the situation!" This makes God big enough to cope with Old Testament problems that had to do with the Red Sea, a fiery furnace, and Noah's ark; but hardly up to date with the space age. Small wonder we find ourselves constantly reducing God to nothing more than a magnified man.

God does not interpret our space explorations, nor other scientific investigations as threats to His omnipotency, nor should we. If any real concern or worry is to be evidenced such energy ought to be directed toward attaining greater insight into the meaning of real faith with less emphasis upon the mere intellectual concept which is so often equated with it. Real faith permits one to "see" God, whereas faith that comes only by hearing of the ear keeps God at a distance. The book of Job illustrates our point.

When Job first began his trials he had only heard of God via the ear, (intellectual concept) but after he had experienced many ordeals with God as a genuine partner, his "ear faith" turned into "power faith." When his ordeals first began and his faith seemed inadequate, we find Eliphaz the Temanite pointing out to him the difference between faith to counsel by and faith to live by.

It vividly points up the difference between what today is nothing less that the "cult of positive thinking" versus the reality of successful life experiences with God. In Job 4:3-6 Eliphaz told Job "You have yourself set many right and put strength into feeble souls; your words (note—words) have kept men on their feet, the weak-kneed you have nerved. But now that your own turn has come, you droop; it touches you close, and you collapse. Let your religion reassure you. . . ." (Moffatt) No doubt, Job tried this and all other formulas he may have possessed, but it was only after he had *actually experienced things with God* that he truly discovered Him and "SAW Him." In Job 40:5 he says, "I had heard of thee by hearsay, but now mine eyes have *seen* thee." Spiritual insight if you please.

And so it is today. Those who have merely read of God and his Old Testament exploits find themselves with a "hear-say" God as did Job, while others who like Abraham, Moses, and David have actually worked with the Creator, eagerly await further and even greater discoveries of the Eternal One. Thus, with the space age upon us let us not find it a time for drooping but an opportunity for challenge, and the reassurance of our faith. Let us quietly repose in the assurance of these words: "God says, Through all the long delay I am still ruling in my justice. When men melt in panic, I still uphold the order of the world." (Psalms 75:2-3) (Moffatt)

—Discovering More of God via Nature—

Actually, one of the very first commands given to man embraces the conquering of the universe. We read in Genesis 1:28, "And God blessed them and God said unto them, Be fruitful and multiply, and replenish the earth and *SUBDUE IT.* . . ." To the writer, this includes everything from conquering dandelions to outer space. All of it amounts to a greater discovery of God via nature and her laws, wherein the bigness and greatness of

His Majesty are further expressed. We don't make God's laws—we simply discover them and at the same time make additional discovery of Him. For example, the student of anatomy and physiology at once has his mind arrested and pointed toward the Genius who made the human body. His appreciation of the words of the Psalmist, "I am fearfully and wondrously made . . ." is greatly enhanced. Moreover, all such discoveries make it possible for the seeker to make even greater discoveries relative to both self and Maker. These and other wonders of nature are so great that man is humbled as he discovers them—and rightly so, because humility and meekness are indeed prerequisites to learning. Jesus so stated with the words: "Blessed are the meek for they shall inherit the earth." (Matthew 5:5) The meek person is both teachable and receptive. Jesus did not mean that the reticent and timid would some day own the earth. In fact, his teachings point to just the opposite.

For example, every *true* scientist is by nature a meek person. This statement possesses truth with a vengeance. That is, he seeks, probes, receives, is passive as well as active, and thus he learns. He doesn't try to make the laws, but meekly seeks to discover them. Moreover, he is pliable and flexible and always ready to modify or change any previously held views as it appears such are unworkable. Truly, he is a receptive person. On this basis then of receptivity and learning, the beautiful scenery belongs to the artist, plant life to the botanist and the secrets of the underground to the geologist. On this same basis, spiritual truth belongs to the meek individual who possesses but a poverty of knowledge and truth—*BUT KNOWS IT!* This is the poverty of spirit listed by Jesus as also being a prerequisite to receiving the kingdom

20

of God (Matthew 5). The humble mind helps create the needed meekness (teachableness) so necessary to learning. Obviously, the superior minded individual is destitute of meekness (teachableness and receptivity) even though he may mask his superior attitudes with a little shyness or self depreciation as needed.

— Study of Nature in Youth Camps —

Just here we feel compelled to inject the thought that Christian Youth Camps would certainly be making no mistake in emphasizing more and more nature study. This might inspire more genuine awe and less mass psychology as perhaps evidenced in herd baptisms. The 19th Psalm would take on new meaning for many, and the humility created by such studies, the finiteness realized, and the insights gained; would be of inestimable value in a new approach and restudy of the entire Bible. *The student would have more tangible evidence of his invisible means of support.* He would feel that his God is up to date and equal to any situation. It hardly seems consistent to tell our children about the young lad David who, with God's help killed a giant, and then leave them with the impression that God knows very little about rockets and space. It will be rather disappointing for the youngster to grow up believing that his God who was "on the ball" in Old Testament times, can hardly be interested in a young man who wants to fly to the moon rather than wade through the Red Sea. He might just doubt if such a God is interested in this era and able to fit into modern life and therefore leave Him behind. On the other hand, if our minds can conceive of God as being interested in our investigations of His universe (and maybe with a twinkle in His eye at that) such might at least lend a tendency toward our viewing Him as being up to date. This concept would make it likely that we could then conceive of the Father as being good companionship for everyday life, rather than some sort of an archaic psychological sedation for funerals.

— Necessity of Seeing God —

It is absolutely necessary that every Christian "see" God in the largest and best conceptions possible. He who fails here limits his own growth and maturity. And just here let us say that the awesome task of preachers and teachers in helping others to do this is enough to make any person who is cognizant of the responsibility cry as did Isaiah, "Woe is me for I am undone . . . *"My eyes have seen the King, the Lord of Hosts."* (Isa. 6:5) It was after the prophet saw the King and then looked at himself that his poor soul cried out as it did. The prophet may have had a fairly good self-image before the King was clearly focused, but afterwards he saw just how badly out of spiritual focus his frail being appeared. Peter perhaps experienced about the same thing when beholding the Master's faith and His drawing upon the resources of heaven. When at Christ's command Peter and others launched out into the lake and lowered their nets they got results even though all previous attempts were failures. At this closeness in working with Heaven, his anguish of soul caused him to fall down at the knees of Jesus and exclaim, "Depart from me Lord, for I am a sinful man." (Luke 5:8) Here Simon saw himself as never before; and likewise, our looking at self will either inflate us until we pop or reduce us to dust and ashes—depending upon what we see.

The individual who simply sees God as a mere magnified image of self (projected self-image) will necessarily have a reduced God. As we reduce God we automatically short change ourselves in everything related to Him. In other words, the person who grasps very little of God will consequently see but very little significance and importance concerning all aspects of His kingdom. This is verified by a beatitude of Jesus, "Blessed are the pure in heart for they shall see God." (Matt. 5:8) The illustrations just given point up the fact that as one's heart becomes less and less filled with self, the more room there is created for entrance and dwelling by God.

— Results of Seeing Him —

Isaiah's need for self cleansing was symbolized by the angel's touching his lips with the hot tongs after which he felt cleansed and ready to approach God and His program. Peter "vented" at the feet of Jesus as part of his catharsis. As aforestated, both saw more of God as their hearts became purer. For these and other reasons, we are of the opinion that the beatitude just quoted does not imply that only after death will the pure in heart see God. We feel that it also includes the import that the pure in heart see Him through faith and spiritual concepts as the inner man is renewed day by day, and as Jesus is spiritually reincarnated within the souls of humble followers. Followers who, like his mother Mary cry aloud in their living for Him, "My soul doth indeed magnify the Lord." There is no wonder that Paul speaks of such souls as constituting a colony of heaven (Phil. 3:20 Moffatt) Such are both continually and continuously experiencing spiritual metabolism (cleansing and renewing) and transforming into the same likeness as Himself passing from one glory to another. (2 Cor. 3:18—

23

Moffatt) Incidentally, this all emphasizes what almost everyone knows—*conversion is not just an event but a process*. In the process the Christian gradually sees more and more of God as promised in the beatitude. This is in tune with song of Mary which bespoke an enlargement of her soul for God and His greater meaning to that soul. Always, the greater our "vision" of God, the greater our results with Him.

— Formation of Concepts (Fear) —

As previously mentioned, the person whose concepts of God are juvenile and perhaps projected, will of necessity be woefully limited in Christian perspective in every sense of limitation. Perhaps, too few of us understand that some of our conceptions of the Heavenly Father are formed via the parental image. This is understandable when we consider for a moment how a child views the parents. To a child the parents are practically omnipotent—thus Godlike. They can solve every problem pertaining to food, security and pain in ways that appear to the child as magical. Every need is met in ways the child cannot comprehend. He interprets this as above him—thus "supernatural." Unless these concepts are greatly altered he will probably correspondingly visualize the Heavenly parent in relation to the same needs. On the other hand, if his father was a very strict disciplinarian who thrashed a child at the least infraction and showed neither understanding, forgiveness, nor flexibility, the child may make the transference to his Heavenly Father, in whom he sees "the boss with the stick" waiting for the least infraction to be committed. This creates fear, but not the fear (awe and reverence) desired by God. This wrong type of fear actually creates resentment and hate,

24

yet causes us to attempt to serve God because we are scared.

— Love Casteth Out Fear —

John nailed that when he said, "Perfect love casteth out fear." (I John 4:19) Why didn't John say that perfect love casteth out hate—it is the antithesis of love, not fear? Because fear is the enticer of hate! This is true in every realm and application. The business man who fears that the other fellow may competitively out-do him and make him suffer is likely to build up unconscious or even conscious resentment toward his competitor. An athlete may do the same if a teammate beats him out for the squad. He rationalizes his loss and perhaps sublimates or represses the resentment. Preachers could also succumb to some of these same things if they should interpret the success of others as threats to their position, popularity or security. In our own experiences it has been our opportunity to note that in practically every patient where unconscious resentment or hatred was uncovered, the patient usually also feared the party. This is particularly true in cases involving children with regard to parents and siblings.

The fear and monster concept breeds frustration and at the same time potentiates certain scriptures which may be construed as fitting into certain legalistic concepts. For example, those who possess these concepts find more fear generated, yet a legal proof text in such scriptures as James 2:10 "for whosoever shall keep the whole law, and yet offend in one point, he is guilty of all." Not understanding the point James is making to Jewish converts (works must accompany faith—get going) these sensitive and fearful souls hold forth this text as an ex-

25

hortation that we must all be one-hundred-percenters. (However, in some places we have noticed that this 100% concept holds true with doctrinal issues but is greatly relaxed when dealing with moral ones. That is, the worship (public) must be 100% correct whether the life tallies with godliness or not.) But anyhow, the 100% concept begets so much unnecessary fear in some hypersensitive souls that one exclaimed in Bible class, "Sometimes I just wish I had died the very minute I was baptized."

This type of fear cheats the possessor at every turn. He will find it very difficult to acclimate himself to even approaching One whom he fears will upbraid him for the approach. Like Mordecai and Esther, in their dealings with Ahasuerus, "No one knows whether the sceptre will be extended or not." Everyone recognizes the tragedy of a child's not being able to converse with his parents, and it is worse than tragic for a child of God to feel unable to do so. Furthermore, where such spiritual intimacy is lacking there can be no real boldness even when the throne of grace is finally but reluctantly approached. It is obvious what havoc such fear can wrought in the prayer life and the entire spiritual development. We have wondered if this uncalled for fear is another reason why so many prayers are nothing but parroted verbalizations rather than desires and needs of the soul expressed to a Father whose greatest delight is to see His children happy? Is our apparent resourcelessness due to our being scared to draw upon the resources of Heaven? More about this when we deal with the Lord's prayer.

— Hypersensitivity to Scripturalness and Results —

If we see God as the monster of heaven, a needless

hypersensitivity toward being scriptural is also created. This type of legalism inevitably binds and limits God (by His own rules) to where He cannot work. It causes us, like the Pharisees, to be guided by the concept that man was made for the Sabbath instead of the Sabbath for man. It causes us to obey certain laws and texts rather than general principles. As a result we find ourselves suffering from *paralysis by analysis*. While stressing scripturalness, we analyze until we paralyze. The result of this is observed in many diversified expressions. For example, the calamity is seen when we become so paralyzed that certain phases of the work of God practically stops—*cold*. While some of us are straining out scriptural gnats, yet swallowing *caravans of camels,* the opportunities pass and we find ourselves yet in a state of inertia. Apparently we would rather discuss the rules than play the game. Is it any reason that in many cases the people so to speak have left their stadium seats in disgust and disappointment while we as both players and umpires eternally discuss the rules? Is it wisdom to understand that a thirsty dying man on a desert is not interested in the formula for water (H_2O) *he wants a drink!* The cries of the world are comparable and we must answer them. And, incidentally, the only destructive act of our Lord that we can recall was that of His smiting the barren fig tree. It's results were nil—it didn't produce! Hence we should take to heart the fact that any movement that is not grounded and geared to the concrete accomplishment of results is doomed when it starts. We must provide the drink, not the formula! The fearful, one talent man, was not only an insult to God—he was practically worthless (unprofitable) because he was afraid and therefore did nothing. The fearful, like the ignorant, always prostitute life. Indeed, fear and ignorance are constant companions in our everyday parade and dress.

— Double Fear Vs Poise of Christ —

While we are noting the effects of fear in relation to the work of the Lord, there is another aspect of it that emerges just here. We refer to the modern method of raising funds for evangelism with the cry, "While I am talking and pleading with you for this money, hundreds of souls are dying and going to hell because they haven't heard the truth." Here we observe double fear at work, but suffice to say it gets results. With reference to such frantic pleas we pose this question: "Just how on earth could Jesus maintain his quiet poise and balance with reference to the need for evangelization while every minute hundreds and thousands were dying and going to hell?" Yet everyone will agree that He had enough on His mind to drive the average person into a catatonic psychosis. Were not the issues as burning at that time? If so, why didn't He work a little differently? He didn't appear to be rushed, though always busy. Perhaps this busy, yet calm and poised life of His can be accounted for if we could entertain for a moment the thought (perish it) that Jesus might not have interpreted *real guilt and sin* as we see it. He might not have viewed everyone as sectarian, or heathen and therefore lost. The Jews did but He didn't! Could it be that both God and His fellowship are quite larger than we have heretofore dreamed possible and have therefore always included some who sustained a divine relationship via love and grace in lieu of "law and scriptural worship?" If we could understand, as did Jesus, that each of us sustains a personal and not a herd relationship to God, and that our

28

relationships and responsibilities are both related to opportunities and capabilities as interpreted by God alone; we might be able to appreciate why Christ worked as he did and consequently we could perform accordingly. This could help us understand the delay of the church (from His death until Pentecost) although it must appear as an eternity to those who can become nothing short of frantic with reference to the thousands who must have died during that period of time. Frantic, because they fail to understand that God has always had a covenant with His people. (The writer has often been asked why Jesus seemed to delay the sending of the apostles. Why he did not quickly give them the Holy Spirit and say "Get going!")

Imagine, if you can, one's frustration together with possible self projection into the apostles as they tarried there in the upper room, torn between the "obsession to go" and the "compulsion to wait." Our purpose in touching on these lines of thought is not to dampen true zeal, but to perhaps uncover it. Not to lessen interest in mission work and the support thereof, but to focus attention on what may be nothing short of foreign proselyting instead of *real mission work*. Frankly, it bothers us just a little every time we hear some zealous brother remark that he is going to some place, where he says, (believe it or not.) "there's not a single Christian to be found." Yet after he arrives should he suffer an acute appendicitis it is always one of those "unregenerated sectarian" medical missionaries who removes his appendix while some nice, "but not-a-Christian" nurse waits upon him (she's sectarian too, you know,) in a hospital that "unregenerated sectarians" built before both he and his religious movement were born. It comes with poor grace for people to come along claiming missionary work in places where the *real* missionary work was perhaps done hundreds of years ago. It could be that some of us are slightly confused with reference to the meaning of genuine missionary work and the real needs of the world. But our concepts of a God who can work only with us and no one else can produce just exactly what we have described, and in abundance.

Needless to say, some fear is a necessity of normal living, but our response to it need not be out of proportion to the stimulus. Nor, should the stimulus be a distortion of fact due to myopic appraisal. The use of fear to raise funds for missionary and other religious work is the utilization of the wrong stimuli. Love will always do the job—it never faileth (I Cor. 13:8).

— Sinners Cannot Run Away —

When God came to our planet in the person of Jesus Christ, He was referred to as dwelling among us full of grace and *reality* (John 1:17 Moffatt) The King James Version says "Full of grace and truth." Hence, truth is reality.

In that day, as now, reality was not always acceptable. Many tried to escape Him (The True Reality) and finally some tried to kill Him—but He returned in three days to proclaim the reality (truth) concerning death. They could neither escape nor kill this Reality, so consequently more and more of them saw the wisdom of accepting Him. Those who felt otherwise continued to run from it, deny it, and even fight it. But the sometimes slow, yet certain consequences show that such attempts at escape will not work. We had just as well attempt to repeal the law of gravity as to try to reverse the laws of God! As stated elsewhere, the laws of God are written within our very being and sin (literally translated—"missing the mark") is nothing short of attempted denial and repudiation of their realism. It cannot possibly work because it misses the mark! This is readily appreciated when sin is reduced to the absolute—that is; when everyone is a liar, everyone is a thief, everyone is a murderer, everyone is a fornicator. When these are practiced in the absolute, chaos comes—everything falls! Reverse this and let everyone be truthful, honest, without hate, and true to their love, and then imagine the difference. The practice of sin then isn't just a matter of badness—it is a continual missing the mark which is accompanied or later followed by frustration, uncertainty, insecurity and ultimate defeat. Defeat in this world and permanent defeat in the hereafter.

If the world should align itself with Truth (Reality) our problems would almost altogether disappear. But again, a part of the problem is that most everyone wants the world saved, (especially their loved ones) but few want the salvation or deliverance to begin with them.

It is stupid to wish and even pray for world peace, and then knowingly try to run away from the methods or rules that produce it. Similarly, it is just as stupid to desire to enjoy life and at the same time rebel and attempt to avoid the rules of truth or reality by which it is to be lived. Aligning ourselves with the laws and purposes of the Creator is not only being good—it is definitely being smart!—It pays. One's disgust, disappointments and disillusionments in life can cease when he decides to stop "missing the mark through sin" and start hitting the bull's eye with Reality—God!

Chapter 2

— Christians Cannot Run Away —

People usually think of preachers as men who walk with God rather than attempting to run away from Him. The Book of Jonah presents one of the exceptions in a most fascinating and meaningful pageantry. While the reader will find this book frankly somewhat amusing (as he witnesses "Jonah's antics," along with his pouting, frustrations and childish reactions) at the same time one will note that it ever bristles with the futility and seriousness of trying to run away from God. Moreover, it serves notice that every life has the most sacred purposes, and that God in some way or other issues challenges and responsibilities along with capabilities by which every responsible human being is expected to dignify both the purposes of life and its Giver.

Jonah was a prophet or a teacher of God. In turn he was asked of God to go to Ninevah and preach to them of their wickedness. It is not fully revealed as to why Jonah rejected this mission, but the book more than hints that the preacher was of the familiar type who are usually quite willing to see the world evangelized if the movement doesn't have to begin with them. He was like his Jewish brothers in Christ's time. They cried, "Hosanna —Hosanna—(save us—save us—meaning their nation)— but none would say "start it with me!" Jonah was not one to take hold of the plow handles and start.

— His Flight —

The reader will note in another chapter our discussion of how we react to various threats and crises by what is commonly called "fight or flight." And to this Jonah was no exception. His was flight. The scriptures read: "But Jonah went away to fly to Tarshish *from the presence of the Eternal*—he came down to Joppa and when he found a ship he *paid the fare* and went on board to reach Tarshish (Spain perhaps) *avoiding the presence of the Eternal.*" (Jonah 1:2-3—Moffatt) These words describe the beginning of "Jonah the Tourist" in a manner almost comparable to that of "One Way Corrigan" of a few years ago. Jonah reacted as though he believed one advanced while in reverse. Obviously nothing could be more stupid. The world is fast discovering that no one runs away from God. His laws are immutable and are for the good of mankind—they are the rules for the game of life and we either play by them or we just don't play.
Instead we pay. Whatever the realm, whether the sciences, religion, arts or what have you, the rules are inexorable. We accept them and in turn get acceptance or we can reject them and get rejected. Consider the polygraph (lie detector) as an example. When truth is told it simply says that the body (nerves, blood, tissue etc.) agrees with truth. When a lie is presented, the same body quickly says "You are throwing everything into reverse and we won't pass it by without strong protest." In other words, our attempts to operate contrary to the laws of God, are nothing short of trying to reverse the normal processes of life. It won't work. It is for this reason that we have stated elsewhere that sin is not only *wrong*, but equally *stupid*. Our text states that Jonah paid his fare, and as one reads the account he sees it as a "whale" of a fare!

— The Storm —

"But the Eternal flung a furious wind upon the sea, there was a heavy storm—Now Jonah had gone below and was lying fast asleep." (vs. 4-6 Moffatt) It appears that Jonah was endeavoring to dissociate himself from God by sleep, but while he slept the storm was mounting. No man sleeps away his problems—it only postpones them until he awakens once again to the same storm with a sudden jar. He cannot sleep them off, drink them away, nor tranquilize them out of existence. They must be met and dealt with. Indeed, this is a part of normal and sane living. The storms abate only when solved, not when denied or postponed.

— Confession And Crises —

The record further relates how Jonah was awakened and his attempted escape discovered and admitted. With this he was asked, "What are we to do with you to make the sea calm?" His reply was, "Take me and throw me into the sea"! Be it said to his everlasting credit, here is the only account of which we have knowledge where a preacher frankly admitted, "Get rid of me and everything will be calm." May this serve as some "spiritual amazement" to the many gracious elders, deacons and even congregations who may have heretofore wondered if such a thing could actually happen.

The story continues with Jonah being cast overboard and swallowed by a whale. Needless to say when one, is "in a whale of trouble" he is likely to pray—and Jonah did. In chapter 2:7 he said, "when I lay fainting, I remembered the Eternal"— (Most likely Ninevah too). After three days and nights the whale vomited Jonah up on the seashore. The writer has often chuckled as he tried to visualize the prophet standing there on the beach watching that whale spout and swim away. Or, maybe Jonah hit the beach making tracks! Anyway, God soon asked him once more to go to Nineveh and the record states that "he arose and went." He now partially realized the importance of playing the game God's way and no doubt forever learned that no man can run away from God. As a result of his preaching to the people of Nineveh, the city was spared including the cattle.

— Reactions —

"When God saw what they were doing and how they turned from their evil life, God did relent—he decided he would not inflict the punishment he had said he would inflict upon them—This vexed Jonah mightily. (3:10 Moffatt) Note, if you please, that here is a preacher, a presumed man of God, greatly vexed because he attained successful results in saving people. Unusual, yes, but not for an "immature pouter." While pouting and grumbling, Jonah actually told the Lord "I knew thou wast a gracious and pitiful God, slow to be angry, rich in love and ready to relent! Now then, O Eternal, take away my life—Better death than life." (4:2-3) To which the Lord asked, "Dost thou well to be angry"? Reader, observe now a man, a grown man, if you please, who poutingly says, "See, I knew you would—and if I can't have my way I would just as soon die." After which God's question was directed as to ask, "Jonah, does it do any good for you to get angry about it"? And again—"Mad enough to die."

— Whoopee—A Gourd! —

Jonah then went out to the city limits to see what would happen to the city. (The writer would not have been surprised had he tacked up his sign and started his own congregation. They have been started for less.) But anyhow, while sitting out there in the heat, God caused a gourd (likely with large leaves) to spring up to shade him. "Jonah was mightily glad of the gourd." (4:6) But next morning God made a worm which gnawed at the gourd till it withered. At sunrise God sent a sweltering east wind, the sun beat on the head of Jonah till he fainted and wished to die. (4:7-8) "Better death than life," he cried. Then God asked Jonah, "Are you right to be angry over the gourd?" "Yes," said Jonah, "Mortally angry" (as we would say "mad enough to die") .

— Lowering the Boom —

Then the Eternal said to him, "You are *sorry about the gourd*—. Am I not to be sorry for that great city, Nineveh?" If it will not seem frivolous and shocking to the reader, the writer would like to share his first impression of some years ago when he observed Jonah's reactions with reference to the gourd. Our thoughts were, "No one, but a spiritual gourd-head could become so emotionalized over a gourd, yet snore in the bottom of ship while a city is going to hell."

Believe you me, it is this same type of church folk who today can become just as worked up over the same things in relation to the Kingdom of God, yet never become excited or too concerned about those things that really count. There is indeed a difference with pronounced distinction between those who religiously "major in gourds" and those who major in cities—cities of souls. God has known it all along, and more and more Christians are catching on. We have finally made the discovery that even as church members we cannot run away from *simple and natural truth*. To pervert the beautiful and simple undergirding of natural truth (reality) and become "Pharisaical lawyers," "Bible technicians," and "scriptural legalists" is to make the plain simple religion of Jesus Christ a system of complexity. As with Jonah, God is slowly but surely lowering the boom of reality upon us. He is simply showing us that we either cease our "paralysis by analysis" and get on with the work of the kingdom or we too will experience a "whale of disillusionment" produced by the poverty of our results. Nothing is more pitiful nor contradictory than a person or movement loudly proclaiming a wealth of means and truth but contradicting it with a drouth of accomplishments!

In our opinion, these important truths should also be recognized and accepted by the church in order to avoid further spiritual abortions in those whom we induce to embrace Christ and His kingdom. People who have finally seen the futility and stupidity of sin and have consequently accepted The Way of Life are neither desirous nor ready to start all over again with what we might call "church merry-go-rounds." They did not accept Christ just for forgiveness and redemption from the *guilt* of sin alone—they were likely told that He delivers from the *power* and *paralysis* of it as well. *To bring intelligent people into the Kingdom of God and then frustrate them with petty conflict, silly interpretations, superficiality of concept and teaching, is sure to be interpreted by them as tendencies on our part toward crowning them as spiritual "gourd heads."* This they will not stand for. They have already seen the nonsense of trying to run away from God (before they became Christians) consequently, any system of interpretation and practice that appears to

37

undermine the *realism of the gospel* will be interpreted by them as difficult and unmeaningful spirituality—yet branded by us as New Testament Christianity. People will choke on this only for a short while—no longer!

SUMMARY

Prior to the sailing of Christopher Columbus, the Spanish Coat of Arms was engraved with the words: "Ne Plus Ultra"—meaning "There is nothing Beyond." After his discoveries, they dropped the "Ne" leaving it "Plus Ultra"—"There is Something Beyond."

It is hoped that another "look" at the Eternal will likewise cause us to expand both our limited thought and conceptual horizons, and in so doing receive fresh courage and faith with which to see and meet all challenges as unfolding opportunities for more discoveries of God. Unfoldings by which we may increase our stature, mature attachment, and identification with Him.

Chapter 3

THE BIBLE

The Bible is the way of life *exposed* and not simply
the laws of God *imposed*. While it is indeed a revelation,
it is more than that. It also contains a divine *record* of
The Divine Revelation—Jesus Christ. This is especially
true of the four gospels. (Matthew, Mark, Luke, and
John.) In these we witness a first hand panorama of the
great invasion of God into the human life. If for no
other reason, it would seem that if we momentarily entertain this concept of the gospels, such would merit
our restudy and evaluation for greater insight as to how
God himself viewed the business of life and lived it.
The Bible by its very nature is abstractual and this pre-
disposes its readers to certain limitations of comprehension. The nearest exception to this is in these four gospels where one is permitted to visualize the life of
Christ and his integration of human life with heaven. In
Christ we are able to see things in the concrete rather
than abstractually. To illustrate, we mean that one is far
more able to see and evaluate real estate by visiting it
and inspecting it than by just reading the abstract de-
scribing it. While admittedly the gospels are descriptive,
they are nevertheless dealing with the absolute concrete
wherein life is depicted at its very best.

Such is hardly the case when one studies the epistles. Having been written perhaps as emergency teachings and advice to correct certain errors of the hour, little opportunity was left for much inspired apostolic supplement to the Great Life. Hence, the greater issues of life as dealt with by Jesus had to give preference to various individual and congregational problems which it appears often constituted of marginal error. While this was of course important, it points up what is stated elsewhere, namely: "All truths are equally true but not equally important." In retrospect the writer partially understands why it appears that the gospels have been deemphasized (unintentionally of course) while Acts and the epistles were given prominence. We are wondering if the approaches and procedures of study used just a few years ago are yet prevalent? They consisted of the study of at least one of the gospels (without correlation with the others) and then a rush off to Acts and the establishment of the church. After this, followed a consideration of the epistles where it appears that we gnawed at the marginal issues of "meat," and other relatively unimportant concepts. As a result, *we majored in minors!* In view of these previous shortcomings, the writer during the past several years has urged a restudy of the New Testament with special emphasis upon the necessity of closely examining some religious premises perhaps heretofore assumed.

For example, the premise that the gospels were written to make believers, Acts to show us how to become Christians and the epistles how to live the Christian life; will most certainly bear reevaluation. Our honest convictions will not permit us wholly to accept this commonly held premise for interpretation of the New Testament. While there is some truth in the premise it is nevertheless, rather shallow and distorting. As already stated, the life, teachings, and work of Jesus give us the best demonstration of those principles to be applied for the integration of man into the harmony of life and the will of The Eternal. Our views permit us only to see the epistles as inspired encouragement and teaching, with some reapplication and adaptation of Christ's principles in the form of corrective measures as the needs arose. Very important, yes, but not equally important in relation to the meaning of the invasion of Christ into human life.

— Influencing Factors —

Naturally, certain sociological and psychological factors along with various cultural patterns were a big consideration as the inspired epistles were written, and such factors are occasionally brought plainly into focus. Obviously, these must be considered with all possible insight if one is to avoid superficialty and some rather unworkable views of related subject matter. Not only this, but possible harm other than disunity, may result if such factors are overlooked. A case in point is that of the missionary who found the native women naked from their waists up. Embarrassed at such "immodest apparel" he hurriedly wrote home to the ladies sewing circle to send him several dozen armless white capes, plus a few hundred yards of white material for native sewing. Imagine his chagrin when the women later appeared in white but with well rounded holes exposing their breasts as usual. Perhaps this preacher was trying to Americanize before he Christianized. To the rigid and inflexible mind who believes right is right wherever it is and that "modest apparel means modest apparel" *universally,* such a predicament would precipitate his working up a spiritual lather. Missionaries could well consider the above incident as they approach polygamy and similar problems.

— Truth Is Fixed But Our Knowledge Is Relative —

While we all recognize that eternal truth is for all ages, we fail to recognize that some first century adaptations and applications for certain cultural patterns are not necessarily binding forever. In our opinion the teachings concerning modest apparel, (of that day) long and short hair, head coverings, and enrolling the widows under sixty, are a few examples that have to be evaluated in view of the factors just mentioned. Unless these and similar texts are considered in fairly accurate background, their general scriptural tenor and purposes will be obscured. Simplicity will have become turned into complexity! Such texts also further evidence the fact that our interpretations of the sacred writ are often based upon various unconscious factors that are as unknown to most of us, as are the unconscious automatisms in the neurotics who are predisposed to sudden and overwhelming conversions, visions and hallucinations. We overlook the fact that many of our religious concepts were created for us by our religious fathers and handed down by tradition. I am aware that many will scream at our even suggesting such ideas, but every person with any insight at all will recognize the relative accuracy of the statement. Of course we all recognize the sincerity of heart in the individual who honestly feels that he is interpreting altogether on his own, because he is wholly unaware of the variety of stimuli that is constantly bombarding him as he weighs his views.

— Harm of Oversimplification —

It will be seen then that such unawareness could have a tendency to make us oversimplify, which is dangerous; and that such possible oversimplification usually comes from the superficial thinker. This is attested by the fact that any superficial thinking preacher can give you a sure and quick formula for religious unity. "Just let the Bible be the guide," he will say, which he is likely equating with "Be reasonable—see it my way." Or he may use an even more familiar one, "Speak where the Bible speaks and be silent where the Bible is silent." It's that simple!! Yet we have so miserably failed in doing just that, that we are here reminded of what an acquaintance stated he saw in Russia a few years ago. In big letters it read; "The Committee for the Rural Electrification of All Russia." Just below the electric door buzzer was a small sign which read, "Buzzer out of order—Please knock." No religious people in the Protestant world has claimed more via a slogan and more miserably failed in keeping it. We have so pitifully failed to speak in countless instances where the Bible speaks, and only heaven could record the times we have come forth with some silly impractical interpretation and application which have amused some of our more enlightened and spiritually minded neighbors, yet evoked their pity. We believe that it was President James Garfield who was wise enough to forsee the incalcuable harm that would come from the slogan, "Speak where the Bible speaks and be silent where it is silent." Undoubtedly, we would have been far better off had that slogan not been introduced. As President Garfield predicted, it did inevitably help cause division among a sin-

43

cere people—a people who like this author are perhaps in need of more insight. The author feels that we should modify the slogan to read: "We *try* to speak where the Bible speaks," etc. His preference, however, would be that we forget it, altogether. Yet, if we just must have one, let it be Christ-centered, rather than Book-centered. We favor *genuine* "Christ-olatry" over superficial "Bibli-olatry."

— Some Expressions of a Slogan —

The "one cup" segment takes the slogan for exactly what it says and are quick to inform us that to speak as the Bible speaks is to say "cup" and not "cups." The brother who wants an elder to have "children and not just one child" (and incidentally, a rather prolific wife) uses the same application. We also heard of a case where a sincere brother objected to a baptistery because of it constituting unscriptural water. When asked why it was unscriptural he replied that it wasn't *"certain water."* When again asked what he meant, he referred to Acts 8:36 where it records that Phillip and the eunuch "came to a certain water." A baptistery he exclaimed was indeed not certain, it could "bust" and run out all over every-thing!—Selah! Ridiculous, of course, but such superficial concepts of the aforementioned slogan and the necessary conclusions therefrom produce such interpretations. It is just such narrowness all the way up our ladder of inter-pretation that causes so much harm in so many ways. It has boomeranged just as President Garfield predicted, because too many uninformed people, simply don't know what they are really saying. The examples just men-tioned, again remind us of the dangers of oversimplifica-tion, and superficial though which is the father of it.

And just here let us hasten to add that if it appears we are indicting some of our reformers or restorers for the slogan heretofore mentioned, we hasten to remind the reader that a midget standing upon the shoulders of a giant can see further than the giant.

But back to the truth and our comprehension of it. As aforestated, truth is fixed and eternal but our knowledge is relative or limited. We don't always act as though it is. This is evidenced by our readiness to condemn an infallible pope (and rightly so) but our willingness to accept an infallible self. Perhaps this is another reason why to so many of us, "everything is as plain as day" and those who don't agree with us just "don't want the truth." This self exalting somewhat compares with the individual who equates knowledge with possessing a big library. Both are very deceptive but ego satisfying. May the Lord *forgive and humble* all of us who feel that we have nothing but the truth and *all of it that's worth having*.

Chapter 4

THE BIBLE

— Lord's Prayer —

Another reason for our sharper look at the Bible is the short-sighted results by practically limiting the scope of the four gospels to a biography of Christ, to make believers. These and a few other superficial concepts are seen in a reevaluation of the Lord's Prayer. We refer to that prayer usually referred to as the prayer that Christ taught His disciples. The writer, however prefers to call it the *Lord's prayer*.

We are told the Christians cannot pray this prayer because the Kingdom arrived about 1900 years ago on the day of Pentecost. (Acts 2) Hence, it is added that to offer that prayer would be to pray for something we already have. (Note the words *"already have."*) Frankly, this is one of the most superficial, cheating, and par roted applications we have ever known.

In the first place, if it is not the Lord's prayer then pray tell us just whose it is? Does it belong to Simon, Phoebe or the eunuch? Had copyright laws existed at that time would the authorship and ownership of Jesus been sustained? If you were asked to write a song, wouldn't you sorta' think of it as being yours even though you were sharing it with others? Furthermore, did the Lord impart some suggestions and pleas to the disciples

46

that were borrowed and not his very own? The prayer *is His* in every sense of the word, but in our hurry to get to the ever-long-sought Pentecost and the saving institution concept, the parroted sermon of the kingdom with law, territory, subjects, etc; we dismiss this great prayer as though it was nothing but a rush quickly request for the church to arrive. Hence, we are supposed to feel that when the church was established the disciples relegated this prayer to the category of fulfilled requests.

Today there are legions who are careful to remind us that the prayer of John 17 is to be called the Lord's prayer. The latter is, of course, a personal prayer of Christ for unity and never to be taken lightly. We have the opinion, however, that such unusual interest in this prayer of John 17 is greatly potentiated for certain church people because they may be consciously or unconsciously entertaining a sneaky opinion that Christ was actually saying, "Father, I pray that the people will see things as they really are (it's so plain) and agree with this group and they'll all be one." Jesus had to correct one little group for equating "not being with us" as not being with Him, but the correction hasn't stood. But back to the objection that we can't pray for something we already have.

First of all, this concept is totally equating the church with the kingdom which is erroneous. This places limitations upon the kingdom which God never intended.

— Kingdom Is More Than "Church Institution" —

While we do not believe in a future dispensation, an earthly kingdom, nor anything similar thereto, we nevertheless, hold that we should always be praying for the kingdom to come. This is because the full expression of

47

what Christ meant—cannot, and should not be limited to a so-called institution. The word kingdom certainly connotes the idea of *reign* and it seems to us that our prayer should always be for more and more of the reign of Christ to prevail in the hearts of men. Is it not our prayer and heart's desire that the Christ be enthroned in the hearts of all children as they are born and grow up? Let's avoid the tendency of leaving the impression that since Christ is the King over an institution and we have the institution —we possess all of the kingdom. I suppose we all do it, but it is nevertheless, nothing short of tragic when we enroll God himself in our own little elementary school of interpretative myopia.

— Kingdom's Resources —

Additional insight into the Lord's prayer will be gained by an evaluation of the gift of the kingdom as mentioned in Luke 12:32, "Fear not little flock it is your Father's good pleasure to give you the kingdom." Contextually, this statement is understood when we note that Jesus is attempting to allay the disciple's anxieties concerning heavenly care. He illustrates the Father's love and care via the birds and lilies. He reminds them that they act like the heathen who for all practical purposes have no Father. Finally, he climaxes his assurance with the statement "Fear not (worry not) little flock, it is the Father's good pleasure to give you the kingdom." In other words, don't be anxious, the resources of heaven are yours—use them! This was a very accurate method of telling them that their worry and anxiety was simply measuring the distance between themselves and God. Jesus also empirically realized the satisfaction of drawing on the resources of heaven because He was constantly doing it, yet often unable to get his disciples to persistently try it. It was only because of his constantly tapping the eternal resources above that he was able to be constantly giving and sharing below. The same holds true with us. So, this promise is just a little different, a little more assuring than His simply saying, "Fear not little flock, after all, you do have an institution." Note too, that it is the Father's good *pleasure* to give us these resources. This points up what we have elsewhere stated to the effect that God delights in seeing his children happy.

In connection with the aforementioned prayer as well as with much else we attempt to evaluate, it is our present blind spots that hinder so much. As with the blind man (in Mark's gospel whom Jesus intentionally and gradually healed of his blindness) just so does partial truth like partial vision distort (men as trees walking). Similarly, it is only after clearer vision is attained that we too can see every man clearly. No doubt some interpretative blind spots have heretofore robbed us of some of heaven's greatest assurances as suggested in the Lord's prayer. In this case, a blind spot is equating the Church with all the resources of the kingdom. Recognizing some of these spots, will help us see the universal presence of such hindrances to Christian growth and maturity and the ever pressing need for more light. Light, if you please, from sources other than our own lanterns.

— The Ten Commandments —

Just as we have taken the Lord's prayer too lightly, we have similarly relegated the ten commandments to an equally unimportant place in study and emphasis. A thorough study and analysis of the decalogue would in

49

our opinion literally bring applause from many who have honestly heretofore dismissed this great spiritual under-girding with a remark such as, "We're not under the law." We would recommend it as choice material for Vacation Bible chools, Youth Camps and similar opportunities for study.

Instead of really digging into these great principles and their meaning and application for today (especially for youth) we have in many instances of congregational and specialized study literally scratched around (like a hen for corn) through cheap and shallow workbooks and their "Mary had a little lamb" methods and actually called it teaching. (Teacher: "What did Mary have?" Pupil: "A lamb." etc.) Is there any wonder that many of our children have grown up wholly ignorant of some of the real ingredients of life's problems and the Bible answers? But alas, a further premium is placed upon spiritual juvenility and relative ignorance by offering such superficial stuff to supposedly grownups. At least such offerings help in one way—the identification of those chronologically of age, but who Biblically and spiritually are perhaps yet in their rompers.

Generally speaking, those who usually delight in such approaches and study of the Bible consequently know "facts and figures" such as Methuselah's age—who begat whom, etc.; but very little about real Christianity, and its relation to life. They attain a mass of disorganized knowledge by majoring in "tid-bits" and fringe details. This compares with an anatomist who knows every bone and muscle in the body, but doesn't know whether man is supposed to walk, fly like a bird, or wiggle like a snake!

Chapter 5

THE BIBLE AS GOD'S PSYCHOTHERAPY

— Learn of Me —

One of the most meaningful and psychotherapeutic prescriptions for real living is to be found in what is often referred to as the great invitation of Jesus. Matthew 11:28-30 records it, "Come unto me all ye that labor and are heavy laden and I will give you rest. Take my yoke upon you and learn of me for I am meek and lowly in heart and ye shall find rest unto your souls. For my yoke is easy and my burden is light."

We must understand that Jesus is not promising relief from the toils of life. Inactivity and lethargy are not to be confused with His promise. In fact, He apparently assumes that all of us know that each is to bear the responsibility of life and meet the burdens and trials that come with it. His invitation and promise is "If you will come unto me, I will give you rest." With the promise He did not leave us in doubt as to how He could give us the rest. Strangely enough, He asserted that the promised rest would come by learning and the wearing of His yoke. Usually, we think of rest coming via a cessation of effort and a period of recuperation. Jesus says otherwise. He says it will come to us by LEARNING and using the proper yoke.

51

"Take my yoke upon you and learn of me" was his appropriate way of saying to those accustomed to the proper use of the yoke: "If you fit yourself to life as I have, if you meet it as I do, if you will use my principles, then the task of living will be what it ought to be. I will not exempt you from the ordeals of life but I will show you how to adjust to them and handle them."

This is indeed appreciated when we understand that the yoke used by the peasant was not an instrument of torture, but a harness carefully made to fit the oxen and make the burden lighter. If the yoke fit, the task became easy. If it did not fit, then both the task and the torture of the yoke had to be borne. This is precisely what Jesus had in mind with reference to the person who takes hold of the plow handles and looks back. Jesus said that such a person was not fit for the kingdom. He wasn't fit because he didn't fit into it. He didn't fit because he had not accepted the harness of heaven. He was using his own brand. This is why a half-cross or a half-hearted religion is harder to use than a full one. One is a task, and the other a joy!

Thus to take the yoke of Jesus means to avail ourselves of the resources which Heaven places at our disposal for living. Such is truly learning of Jesus. It all adds up to our learning the way of life as lived by Jesus, taking His way as the harness of heaven, and stepping out into the ploughing of life.

Once again, we are made to see that the teachings of the Bible are not just a means of saving man from the guilt of sin, but also from the power of it. In other words, it will not only point us to the Saviour who will save us from hell hereafter, but one who will also save us from a "living hell" on earth.

Like the oxen's yoke, the yoke or harness of Jesus has been especially made to fit into and work within the framework of life. It's the only thing with which man may harness himself and get a decent fit. The same God who created the game of life, also made the inexorable rules by which the game is to be played. He has a way of saying "Play the game of life by my rules or get hurt." As he told Paul "It is hard to kick against the pricks." It all adds up to what someone has said, "Life is either awfully simple, or it's simply awful." We take our pick!

For these and many other reasons Jesus says to all mankind, "Do it my way, and ye shall find rest for your souls." Thus, every wise individual will accept the Bible as the way of life revealed and study it diligently as God's psychotherapy for everyday life. What sane person doesn't want his life to be happy and thrilling?

THE BIBLE—God's Psychotherapy

— Stupidity of Sin —

Heretofore, we referred to the Bible as the *Way of Life Exposed* rather than just the laws of God imposed. By this we mean nothing less than the applications of the teachings of God for happy, successful daily living. To live in harmony with the teaching of God is not only being good, *it is being smart.* Conversely, failing to do so is not only sin, *it is stupid!* Stupid, because it is an attempt to reverse life as it should be lived and make it work in a way that life's Creator never intended. Imagine if you can, an individual taking a cross-country vacation but attempting to drive with his car in reverse and enjoy the scenery at the same time. This would be ridiculous and man is finally, but painfully, discovering that

53

he cannot reject the teachings of God and really live. We may exist while so attempting, but live—never!

This gives additional meaning to the words of Jesus that "Man shall not live by bread alone, but by every word that proceedeth out of the mouth of God." (Matt. 4:4) *The word is the rule of life.* The world is fast discovering that man is perfectly free to do as he should but not as he would. This is no doubt included in the statement of the Master, "Ye shall know the truth, and the truth shall make you free." (John 8:32) Knowing the truth and living by it frees us of untold problems, and as we shall see later on, it is a reminder again and again that ignorance is not only wrong but a cheater at the same time. The sooner we learn that God's laws, written and unwritten, are as inflexible as the law of gravity, and just as self verifying,—the sooner we will see the wisdom of harmonizing therewith.

INSIGHT NEEDED

"Leave simpleness, and live, and walk in the ways of insight." (Prov. 9;6 R.S.V.) Gaining insight into oneself involves more than acquiring knowledge. Information becomes insight when it is emotionally accepted and integrated by the ego. We might paraphrase the scriptures just quoted as "Don't be a simpleton if you really want to live, gain some insight as to how to really live and walk in it!" To gain this insight we first note that

— LIFE IS RELATIONSHIPS —

One of the first and fundamental lessons one needs to learn for this greater insight is that both life and death are matters of relationships. This is true in every sense of the word from cell life to man's relationships with his Maker. Death is the result of things being out of proper

54

relationship. When cell relationships become too impaired in the human body, death ensues; and the same holds true in the spiritual counterpart. This also points up the fact that *both death and life are relative*. For example, the individual with a completely paralyzed arm is alive but for all practical purposes a part of him is dead. The same may be said if he is unable to hear, speak, or see. He is partially alive, yet partially dead.

In other words, some of his normal relationships are severed and he is partially dead. We may say then that both death and life in the individual depend upon the extent of his normal relationships with his environment. The more he is in harmony or in correspondence with his total environment, the more alive he is. Conversely, the less harmony he sustains with his environment, the poorer the relationships and greater the degree of relative death. It was no doubt upon this premise that Paul spoke of a certain woman (living in pleasure) as being dead while she liveth. (I Tim. 5:6) She was out of spiritual correspondence and harmony with God, the sustainer of life. Likewise, the prodigal son while away, was referred to as being dead. Upon his return to his father he was considered alive. Inasmuch then as God is the creator and sustainer of life, it is evident that one must sustain the best possible relationships with Him in order to really live and enjoy it. Jesus so emphasized when he said, "I am the vine and ye are the branches." (John 15) From me you receive your everyday life. To have the opportunity to do this and refuse to do so is deliberately placing one's self on the level of a lower animal and loving it. Someone has said that man does not say to a hog, "you're a hog," for the simple reason that a hog can never be anything else. With man it is different. He can transform himself into being more like his Maker and less like himself. To do this is really starting to live—it is the formation of proper relationships.

— Living Begins with God —

The beginning place then for real living is God! In Him life holds together, without Him it falls apart. Paul says, "And all coheres in Him." (Col. 1:18 Moffatt) While in depression and a dejected mood (due to poor temporary relations) the Psalmist cried out, 'My health is wasting under my woe, my life is eaten away with sorrow and my years with sighing. My strength gives way under my punishment, my body falls to pieces." (Psa. 31:9-10 Moffatt) (Note that the body falls to pieces—life falling apart.) While we shall have much more to say upon this, suffice now to understand that the rule of life is simply, "Stick together with God or fall to pieces," in every sense of the meaning. In this thing called the business of life and happy living, everything centers around the cohesiveness of God! We either hit the bulls-eye or we altogether miss the target. Proper rlationships mean life, improper ones, relative and *ultimate* death!

— Relations to Others —

Surely, and forever, all of us should clearly understand that our relationships are no better with God than they are with that brother with whom they are the poorest. The idea of one being in spiritual harmony with his God and out of spiritual harmony with his Christian brother is being stupid. Someone has said, "Our love for God is equal to our love for that man whom we love the least." It is upon Biblical premises such as these, that true racial prejudice, social injustices and individual harms are also sins against every man and God Himself. When man fully recognizes his brother as being a part of himself he will treat him accordingly. Jesus so illustrates by showing that man and woman when married (under God) form a union where partial self identity is lost. He said to love the companion was to love self, while to hate, was to hate self. (Eph. 5:28-29) The same is true with reference to our fellowman (both good and bad) because every man has a part of God's spirit (life) in him and is therefore a part of God and His human family. Moreover, this is doubly true with reference to spiritual children of God who possess the gift of the Spirit in addition to the spirit of life itself.

Likewise, in the parable of the good Samaritan Jesus clearly showed that we are our brother's keeper. To love each other is the fulfillment of our greatest rsponsibility to one another and thus fulfills the royal law. Again we point out, that this relationship is sustained only in proportion to our relationship with God. If we are Heavenly eccentric (off center with God) we're always closer to the margin with everything else.

— Handling "Things" —

We likewise sustain a relationship to things. And by things we mean things like money, houses, lands, clothes, cars, etc. It appears that a big temptation of man is to dethrone his God and place "things" and himself upon the reigning throne. Paul nailed it when he said, "For the love of money is the root of all kinds of evil." (I Tim. 6:10) John did likewise when he warned, "Little children keep yourselves from idols." (substitutes) — (I John 5:21) Placing God and His kingdom first relegates "things" to where "things" belong. An interesting sidelight along this line is observed by noting the visit of Jesus in the home of Mary and Martha. (Luke 10:38-42).

While Jesus was in their home, Mary sat at His feet and heard His words. Here was an opportunity to literally assimilate spiritual food, so Mary grabbed it. But Martha, like many of us today, was *cumbered* about with much serving. Jesus said she was careful (anxious) and troubled about many *t-h-i-n-g-s*. "Things" was the net that momentarily caught Martha. It is the same net from which most of us find it so difficult to extricate ourselves. Just the things of daily life, if you please. We have not learned that everything belongs to the man who wants nothing!" Learning this would go a long way toward helping us to know the meaning of being content. Being content takes away the lure and *distorted* value of "things."

Greater and nobler responsibilities can never be given us until we learn to handle the "things" we now have.

— Handling Self —

As noted elsewhere, man is born with inherent drives to satisfy self. We speak of some of them as our ids. It is our duty and responsibility to so integrate, condition and control these basic drives of satisfying hunger, warmth, thirst, sex, security, etc.; that resultingly we can find ourselves acceptable to God, our fellowman and self. In pursuance of these responsibilities, it is our belief that the man who isn't morally and spiritually inhibited hasn't risen very far above the brute level. In fact, this is the everlasting fight between the carnal man and the spiritual. Paul voiced it as, "But I see another law in my members, warring against the law of the mind." (Rom. 7:23) He had previously said, "I cannot understand

58

my own actions, I do not act as I desire to act: on the contrary, I do what I detest. (Rom. 7:15 Moffatt) In an effort to clearly differentiate between the two men (carnal and spiritual) the apostle makes an inspired, but what amounts to a correct psychiatric diagnosis of complete dissociation. Hear him, "That being so, it is not I who do the deed, but sin that swells within me." (Rom. 7:17—Moffatt) But reader, don't forget, man is held strictly accountable for his endeavors toward bringing this carnal man into captivity, because the apostle affirms that *it can be done.* (vs. 25) It won't do for us to run wild, wholly uninhibited, doing as we please and justifying our action with, "It is not I, but the carnal fellow—sin." (In other words—I can't help it) The Lord happens to know the difference between "spiritual" (divided heart) and frank schizophrenia, and unless the last mentioned happens to be the case, its spiritual counterpart won't have a chance at the judgment.

— Cheated —

The worst part of our making ourselves God, is that we get cheated both now and hereafter. The Father in heaven places the kingdom's resources at our disposal, and we stupidly attempt to dethrone Him and depend upon our own. This is so tragic! Tragic, because our resources are so often weighed and found wanting. Being our own god is like trying to pull ourselves out of the problems of life by the hair of our heads. Playing god ourselves involves our finding the "self god" so inadequate. The "self-god" may even be asleep or totally ignorant of the means of rescue. Thus we cannot say as David: "When I was hemmed in thou hast freed me often (Psa. 4:1— Moffatt) because our playing God is actually what is hemming us in. Everyone will see this as being so obvious at the judgment. Even those sinners who remain outside the fold because they see a few hypocrites (play-actors) on the inside will see it. Actually, no church member can ever approach the hypocrisy of the plain unconverted sinner for the simple reason that by trying to live without God he has made himself "authority, knowledge and savior." In every sense he is play-acting in the largest possible scale. He above everyone else is serving his own self cheating and self-installed god—A play actor if there ever was one. And he gets cheated both here and later. Sometimes it is only after some have been "god" for a while and discovered the shortcomings and disappointments that accompany such self deification, that they are willing to dethrone self and enthrone His Majesty. They finally discover that they, like Paul, cannot kick against the pricks. As aforementioned, all coheres in God and everything falls apart without Him. Is there any wonder that Jesus defined both discipleship and its prerequisites as: "If any man would be my disciple let him *deny himself* and take up his cross *daily* and *follow* me." (Luke 9:24) We note that denying self results in our following —not leading nor equating ourselves with Him. Mindful that this chapter deals with God's teachings as psychotherapy and the resulting happiness, we might well conclude this portion dealing with self with a little lesson in anagram which we recall as the joy formula:

> J — esus
> O — thers
> Y — ourself

It will be noted that the formula calls for Jesus first, other secondly, and self—*last!*

SUMMARY

God is the Creator of life and knows how life should be lived. He has revealed this to us via the Bible and its record of Jesus Christ—the best revelation possible. Man needs understanding and insight into these laws of life that he may be happy here and in the world to come. Understanding then that life is a matter of proper relationships, we must learn how to form and maintain them and make any necessary adjustments as the need arises. The better the relationships the richer and happier the life. The poorer these relationships the more impairment of life, or relative death. The following pages will deal in more detail with the Bible as God's psychotherapy for man.

* * *

Note to ministers—This theme will again be dealt with in the last chapter on "Counselling the Emotionally Disturbed."

GOD'S PSYCHOTHERAPY (LOVE)

The greatest force for living and the best therapy for the human race is love. To love, in the real meaning of the term, is to reach the high water mark in real living. Understanding that life is largely that of relationships, we are quick to add that love does more to make these relationships what they ought to be than anything else. As one psychiatrist stated, "Love in our psychic life is the greatest combining force that *seeks to join all parts together*." (Love or Perish—page 38 by Smiley Blanton, M.D.) Now lay that profound psychiatric statement along side these and note the perfect harmony. "All things cohere (hold together) in Him." (Col. 1:17) "God is love." (I John 4:16) Thus love holds everything together. As we shall see, it is by love that we are physically, emotionally and spiritually held together. In other words, love integrates the whole being. We shall also see that without love, we fall apart. That is precisely why society falls apart on a global basis—it begins with the individual. War in the form of world conflict is an expression of it.

WE ARE BIOLOGICALLY MADE TO LOVE

Nothing attempts to arrest the processes of life like our failing to love. The physiology of the body cooperates with us if we love and it protests if we don't. Some years ago we read in a medical journal where some physicians conducted experiments with rats which supports our statement. They simply angered the rats until they were blind with rage and opaque film began to form over their eyes. We are told that a certain species of fish in India responds in about the same way. One can dangle the empty hook before them until they actually turn red with rage and grab the hook. (P.S. They are very small fry, however.) The lack of love places a *stress* upon the body which can show up later in hypertension, arthritis and other symptomatology. We recall having seen in class the film "The Stress and Adaption Syndrome" illustrating the great work of Dr. Seyle. Before one's very eyes as autopsies are performed, evidence of ulcers, arthritis and other diseases are witnessed as products of stress. Much of our human stress and similar consequence are definitely due to a lack of real love.

By real love, we mean a differentiation between real love and the domestication of resentments and hates.

LOVE INOCULATES

Sometime ago our attention was arrested while reading from a European psychiatrist wherein he pointed out that nurses caring for patients confined with typhoid actually registered a much higher immunity in titer agglutination tests due to what he along with others attributed to nothing but genuine Christian love and service. (Christian homeostasis) There is a Christian poise that contributes to what is often referred to as "homeostasis" or balance which is expressed physically, emotionally, and spiritually. This poise results in less stress and definitely contributes to better health.

Just as love actually immunizes one against physical disease, it does even a better job in the spiritual realm. It immunizes us to the digs, gouges, and slights that must necessarily come from immature people as the kingdom grows up. David might have had this needed balance in mind when he petitioned, "Teach me thy way . . . and lead me by a *level* road." (Ps. 27:11) His seeing the "scoundrel whetting his sword." (Ps. 7:12-14) may be another reason why he said, "Fret not, it only leads to evil." (Ps. 37:8) Moreover he also declared, "I faint with moaning . . . trouble wears away my strength . . . I age under the outrages of my foes." (Ps. 6:6 Moffatt) We note that his aging was caused by his foes. The man who has foes, rather than "enemies who are friends" is sure to age. Like David again, "Thou countest up my sleepless hours, my tears are gathered in thy bottle." (Psa. 56:8 Moffatt) Again he declared, "When my *heart was sour* when I felt *sore,* I was a *dull stupid creature,* no better than a brute before thee." (Psa. 73:21-22 Moffatt) All of these point up the effects upon both soul and body when proper homeostasis is lacking and wrong emotions rule.

It was the great love of Jesus that made it possible

63

for Him to always look beyond the indignities committed against Him (spitting in His face, the plots, opposition from immature and ignorant people, plus the petty stuff of his own disciples) and get on with His great purpose of life down here. One can often tell the size of a man by what upsets him, and if this be true we begin to see more and more the size of the Master, and incidentally the spiritual microscopic specks of ourselves. Stephen, along with the apostle Paul and others received nothing less than a spiritual transfusion of love from Heaven, otherwise they might have acted less like Heaven and more like some of us. They knew and experienced the fact that the more love we possess the nearer we approximate Heaven. Because God is love! A strong brotherhood conspiracy of love would do more for us toward attaining unity than any other approach that might be discovered. It would soon cause us to feel, talk, and act, like we were united and discover that we really are. We would not have to champion some particular dogma, defend some special point, lead some brotherhood segment to convince ourselves and others of our great love and stand for the truth. A genuine expression of the real and deeper meaning of love (which few of us have ever touched) would easily convince all thinking people that we have finally grasped this great truth which is the absolute undergirding of all truth. They would see that we know the difference between certain dogmatic or, mere intellectual truth and the deeper realism of it (truth of life) as depicted by Christ in person. Such would give real meaning to what Paul states in Rom. 12:10 "Put affection into your love for the brotherhood." (Moffatt) We would understand this to mean: "Expressions of warm regard, tenderness, devotion, and attachment." In other words,

Paul is saying: "Give full expression to your love for one another by your warm regard, your tender care, and concern, your unquestionable devotion and unbreakable attachment." The author and a few others he has observed, have occasionally translated the above a little differently via their modus operandi—too bad! Right here we are reminded of the words of J. M. Barrie: "Every man's life is a diary. His humblest hour is when he compares the way he actually wrote it with the way he intended."

In view of the inoculation that love gives and the genuine bigness that accompanies it, are we not made to retrospect as to why in bygone years some really "big men" (in the evaluation of Heaven) among us were often sneered at because they couldn't stoop to the immature level of some of us who though these men lacked sufficient conviction to join in our petty fights? They were inoculated by love. It took!

LOVE

— It Never Faileth —

Perhaps the most meaningful scene described in the entire word of God is that of our Lord actually dying on a tree for us. This arrests our minds and challenges every semblance of amazement to be mustered. While this scene is being sharply brought into world focus, accompanying, though less relatively unimportant sidelights are within the depth of field or acute peripheral vision. While man is being permitted to kill his own Deliverer in order that the Divine love may not fail, the same event is appropriately used to demonstrate that the human embodiment of this same type of love would likewise never fail. In other words it is equally powerful and dependable when in human hearts. The only tragedy of love in such hands could only result from a quantitative shortage.

The apostle John (Ch. 19) describes the Crucifixion setting which includes the presence of Mary, the Christ's mother, as an onlooker. Jesus beheld her as evidenced by the words "Woman behold thy Son." In seeing her He also saw her heart. This revealed certain needs of his mother, whereupon He turned to John with "Behold thy mother!" But wait—Mary was not the actual mother of John. Salome was his mother.

At once the spontaneity of John's love was touched and evoked for immediate response. John understood perfectly just as love always does. It has a quality that is even eager to be discovered and put to use.

Unlike Nicodemus, no lengthy explanation had to be made to John. The words "Behold thy mother" were sufficient. It was though Christ had said: "John, my mother is *our* mother when she needs you." The record states that John took her into his own home from that hour. His love never failed! Moreover it was quick to respond, because love is blind to rigidity, precedent, and quibbling. Sometimes it responds to a need even if it has to make a way. It never fails.

Let us now note love as a psychotherapeutic force with its never failing results.

LOVE

— It Never Fails—An Anchor —

Another interesting aspect of love is witnessed in the dynamics of modern psychotherapy. Time and time again in this field one is confronted with the fact

66

that love is a bond and anchor of safety. Previously, we have stated that man is biologically constructed to love. This is further evidenced in the use made of love as an intrapsychic defense mechanism. By this we mean that when people sometimes need to be defended from compulsively performing some cruel or harmful act, it is the unconscious mind that often prevents their doing so, by developing in some cases some type of an obsessive—compulsive defense mechanism which the person will not actually perform. For example, we recall a referral of a few years ago in which the patient related how she was obsessed with the thought of actually harming her child. With tears in her eyes, she said, "God knows I love my child, but why do I have to think of such a thing." Psychotherapy revealed what we had strongly suspicioned, —that of her having intense unconscious hatred with murderous impulses toward someone else. This someone else, the patient consciously loved (she had married him a few years before) but unconsciously hated. To defend her against such aggressive acts of hostility toward the husband, her "built-in-by-the-Master safety mechanism" had transferred or projected these feelings into her child whom she would not actually harm. *Love would hold her!* When these dynamics were explained to her (and she was able to emotionally accept them) the obsessive-compulsive feelings soon left her and she resumed an even healthier life than before.

At the risk of being boresome to professional readers, let us hasten to add that this patient at first interpreted these feelings as punishment from God. A lengthy lecture from the Bible disputing this would have been about as helpful as would an oar to Noah with his ark. We speak this to declare what most ministers perhaps already know—that a general solace from the Bible such as we are all sinners, etc; is by no means a decent substitute for the insight needed by these people. Guidance to the proper therapy is the best approach for any servant of God in these and similar cases. In the meantime all Christians should learn that we are not "immunized" to emotional upheavals and mental illnesses anymore than we are to fractured arms and limbs. More about obsessions and compulsions later.

LOVE

— It Never Faileth — (I Cor. 13:8)

Inasmuch as John has stated that "God is Love" and Paul asserts that "it never faileth"—we must confess that if it were ever shown where real love has once failed; the writer could almost believe God capable of th same. Even under the Old Testament law with its resulting culture and "eye for eye" procedures, love always worked.

In 2 Kings the sixth chapter the account is given of the Syrians warring against Israel. It will be recalled that Elisha prayed that the Syrian army might be stricken with blindness. The Lord granted this request, and as we shall see for very good reasons. With his request granted, Elisha led the Syrians straight to Samaria and into the presence of the king of Israel.

With the enemy helplessly blind, the king desired to kill them and asked Elisha for approval. Instead of approving this act of hate, the prophet commanded that bread and water be set before the enemy that they might eat and drink, and then return to their homes. This was done and the account closes with the words "So the bands of Syria *came no more* into the land of Israel." This act of love was the cure. It was redeeming and healing.

Call the people and their culture of this day blood-thirsty, barbaric or whatever you please, but one thing protrudes like the proverbial sore thumb. Love is a universal law, knowing no races, economic boundaries nor other stratifications in human affairs. It permeates all of them, and not only works—it never fails! Let's observe its wonderful results in another realm of healing.

LOVE

— It Never Fails to Heal —

We have previously illustrated how love served as an anchor to a person with strong obbsessive-compulsive thoughts, and here we risk another account which somewhat reveals it's redemptive and healing effects.

Some years ago the writer was somewhat surprised when a casual acquaintance, a young woman in her late twenties or early thirties, was referred to us with the following problem. She related that she was very nervous (which was clearly apparent) and experiencing both obsessive and compulsive thoughts that were as she stated it "simply driving me crazy!" "In fact, I may already be," she added.

She told of being afraid to either ride the bus or drive to work. Her father had to both take her and come after her. This was because she was constantly obsessed by the thought that she might "lose control" and brutally attack a small child or even a group of them. At noon she took only half of her lunch period at which time she ate in a drug store on the first floor of the office building thus precluding the necessity of venturing forth on the open streets. Immediately after eating she returned to her desk and began her work as a diversonary attempt.

On her first trip to our offices, she had to be accompanied by her father. "She could not risk this distance alone" she stated. Concommitant with these feelings and impulses were frequent feelings and periods of depression. Subsequent interviews revealed the party's very strong fear of recognizing the dynamics or causes of her trouble. It was evident that she was seeking what we (our image) could mean to her, but she was ever on guard against being disarmed. Tediously, we permitted this lady to reveal her history with a minimum of comment and interrogation by the writer.

In time we were finally able to bring her around to talking about her family and interpersonal relationships. We discussed her marriage and subsequent divorce, after which she and her small child made their home with her parents.

Omitting much detail and session content brings us to the cause of her anxiety. As a child, she had never had the best of relations with her mother, nor while in high school and college. Her mother had been extremely over-protective and resented her marriage. So much so, that the patient felt that her mother was the cause for her matrimonial failure. Perhaps enough has already been stated to indicate the strong likelihood of resentment and hostility toward the mother. Subsequent chats revealed that this was exactly the case.

The patient's continual repressed resentment and hostility was greatly potentiated after her marriage ended in divorce, and this indirectly forced her to return to that from which she had so long sought complete emancipation. Thus, she repressed and "stood it" for just so long (a few years) and finally her hostility "broke through" in the form of the psychological conversions (obsessive and compulsive impulses of attacking) and accompanying bodily symptomatology. The mechanism of displacement was used to externalize her anxiety via the abessive compulsions heretofore mentioned.

Due to all of this hostility being unconsciously directed toward her mother, the patient would also experience strong guilt feelings and worthliness. Along with these she occasionally inverted the hostility (toward herself) and consequently had thought of suicide a few times. With all of this, there is no wonder the woman thought she was "losing her mind."

It required more than two months of regular sessions for this woman to arrive at a point where a few of these dynamics could be discussed without too much discomfort. It required even longer for her to recognize her latent hostility and feelings toward her mother. When all we have mentioned (and much detail obviously omitted) was recognized, emotionally accepted, together with some positive steps toward better interpersonal relations; the patient began to live again. Her obsessive-compulsive thoughts and impulses diminished, and she was able to ride a bus to work and walk home.

About this time the writer changed locales and left her in the competent hands of a consultant. The happy conclusion for the the author came when he received a letter some months later, informing us of her satisfactory recovery and thanking us for a "new life." She had found a new life by rediscovering her love for her mother and above all the *Father*.

I am compelled to strongly emphasize to the reader that love is exactly what brought about these gratifying results. We are not overlooking all of the sessions, discus-

sion, listening, culling, evaluation, and "road clearing"
that was necessary to uncover and further develop a heretofore suppressed and arrested love; yet it was only when
the *warmth of love was found* did our case blossom into
recovery and happiness. Love was the answer—it never
failed!

God's Psychotherapy Humility

One of the most profound psychotherapeutic statements in the word of God is "Humble yourselves therefore under the mighty hand of God." (I Pet. 5:6) To
many of us humility means a show of quietness, timidity,
and masked aggressiveness. These expressions serve as a
disguise for the real meaning of it. The Bible teaches that
genuine humility under God is discovered when one
recognizes one's capacities and limitations, and his cor-
responding responsibilities. The highway of life is littered
with the wreckage of people, religious people too, mind
you, who have failed to graps this. Parents have frustrated
their offspring by encouraging or even forcing them to
attempt to operate beyond their capacities. For example,
the mother who wanted to be an organist and couldn't,
"wears both Elvina and the bench smooth" in trying to
compensate for her own disappointment. Elvina doesn't
care a whit about an organ, she wants to study butterflies
or botany. Comparable expressions of our attempting to
stretch beyond our humble capacities are legion, and if
we had to mention one it would be that of preaching.
The church has long neglected her obligation to discourage some of us from preaching. It often proves both
costly and tragic to wait for us to be weeded out by the
"trial method." How often has the reader heard a remark
similar to this: "He is a good man but he just can't

preach." Our Christian colleges have helped here in no little way. They have done a service in discouraging some and providing better training for the others.

Let us again warn of the consequences which almost inevitably follows the stress and strain of one trying to reach beyond his capacities. It places undue strain upon both soma and psyche and the illness follows. We have to share a portion of the guilt for not helping to prevent some of the illnesses that are often precipitated, if not actually caused in well meaning preachers, teachers, elders and others, who are not emotionally equipped for such demanding tasks. Teachings that tend to push people beyond their capacities—resulting in frustrations, conflicts and feelings of guilt and condemnation. Both teaching (Bible school) and preaching have been oversimplified.

Recognizing our capacities does not mean that we cannot enlarge nor improve them, but such recognition takes into account that we evaluate with insight and if necessary with professional objective help.

— Taking A Sane View —

One of the first lessons the Christian must learn is that God is not interested in competition from man's viewpoint. This is indicated in the statement, "Not to think of himself more highly than he ought to think." (Rom. 12:3) Or as Moffatt translates: "He must take a sane view of himself." This admonition is not just to prevent us from playing the smart-aleck but to recognize our limitations. God has given us various gifts or several abilities, and He is satisfied with our honest efforts because such is truly being morally honest and displaying the integrity of life. This recognition helps bring peace and contentment, and prevents undue strain and stress. These in turn promote good health—physically and spiritually. It is in this manner that humility is a part of God's psychotherapy for Christian living.

In this age when man is usually applauded for trying to stretch beyond his normal capacities, we see the payoff in ulcers, constant headaches, nervous tensions and breakdowns. We are here reminded of the findings by anthropologists of a tribe who were evaluating success by a man who had heaped before his hut, the largest "mess" of unused rotten fish. In other words, his success was evidenced by the odor he created.

God's Psychotherapy for Worry

If the reader has not heretofore discovered that God delivers from the power of sin as well as the guilt of it, he is now approaching the threshold thereto. It is unthinkable that God would be willing to save man from the guilt of sin and leave him wallowing around for a life's span in unhappiness. Jesus said, "I have come that ye might have life and have it more abundantly." (John 14 Chap.) The great invasion by Him into human life verifies what He said. It is interesting to note that while Jesus was human and therefore susceptible to life's passions, temptations, frustrations, emotional upheavals, worries, and anxieties, he was a calm, poised, balanced and mature individual. He was life at its very best. Don't entertain the thought "O well, He was the Son of God and that's the reason." While we recognize this factor, we must nevertheless not attribute His success to that a'one, else there would be no lesson for us in His victorious life. His success in life was due to His constantly taking the resources and teachings of Heaven as His own and operating in harmony with them. Our success of effort to approximate His life, and enjoy ours at the same time, will only come when we do the same. If we are able to learn the lessons of Jesus and the Bible with reference to worry, a greater happiness will be ours.

Worry and the results therefrom are about as old as Eden. The wise man said, "Banish all worries from your mind and keep your body free from pain." (Ecc. 11:20 Moffatt) With further emphasis relative to the effects of worry upon health and general happiness, he also said, "A merry heart doeth good like a medicine, but a broken spirit drieth the bones." (Prov. 17:22 Moffatt) Worry then, has been rightly described as the sand in the machinery of life. The author has seen numerous cases of spastic colon, arthritis, rheumatism, migraine and tension headaches that could be partially attributed to worry. The proof is in the fact that such complaints completely cleared up when the worrying ceased. Worrying is perhaps attributable to at least three main causes. (1) Lack of information concerning the problem. (2) How to effectively deal with it. (3) Insufficient faith in God.

Many times we worry about things simply because we have only meager knowledge of the matter. A little knowledge can cause great worry, whereas adequate information will likely dissipate it. For example, when we learn that a loved one is injured but not the extent, we will no doubt worry. If however, we secure all the details along with a physician's confirmation of recovery, our worry abates, or even ceases, and the energy that was used in worrying is directed elsewhere. Shall we say into more profitable channels!

Again, if we are confronted with a difficult problem

75

and feel helpless with reference to the solution, worry is a result. Perhaps financial worries are an expression of such. Likewise marital problems aften present the stimuli for seemingly undue worries. Most all of these could be alleviated or dissipated if we would take a sensible approach to them. For example, in the case of an injured loved one, the answer might lie in the making of a phone call. In the second mentioned case, the answer would apparently be in seeking the proper help and intelligently meeting the problem. In those cases where apparently the solution is altogether beyond our reach, the solution might call for discussion with competent counsel and full resignation unto God. God most certainly expects us to grapple with those problems we are capable of meeting, and He has promised His help where needed. *Sometimes a child's complete helplessness is his greatest prayer for that help.*

Worry in most cases is like our saying to God, "I can't trust you so I'll take over and w-o-r-r-y it out." To worry is to deal with a problem three times,—before it arrives, while present, and after it is gone. *It is nothing short of the Christian's own brand of infidelity.* Jesus told His disciples that their worries and anxieties concerning life were making them act like heathens who for all practical purposes had no God. He also referred to some as having the spiritual life choked out of them by worries. "Getting *choked upon worries, money* and the *pleasures* of life. (Luke 8:14 Moffatt) It would be well to remember that while all three choke—we as a rule condemn the money and pleasures, yet condone, if not actually approve the worrying. All worry is unnecessary because if the problem has a solution it should be sought and diligently pursued until solved. If unsolvable, surrender it to God.

If we fail to do these we will find as Solomon stated, "Worry weighs a man down." (Prov. 12:25)

GOD'S PSYCHOTHERAPY (Inferior feelings)

Inferior feelings reflect feelings of inadequacy toward life's situations. Some of these are due to various forms of fear, guilt and even aggression. The inferior person may be pretty rigid and see quite a discrepancy between what he is and what he thinks he ought to be. He may find himself unconsciously competitive in just about everything. This is sometimes accompanied by resentment, because we usually resent those to whom we feel inferior. Inferior feelings beget jealousy. They are really the result of our not seeing things as they really are, and by our misconceptions of real values. (We are not overlooking the environmental factors, social pressures, demands, etc., because it is these that often create the false standards.)

— THE CURE —

The best permanent cure we know for the inferiority complex is a reevaluation of things. Psychiatrically this cure would partially come through a process known as identification and incorporation. This is a primitive mental mechanism operating outside of one's conscious awareness, in which he takes a part or parts of another person or persons as his very own. Such is sometimes observed when a play, movie or T.V. program so impresses a youngster that he finds himself talking and walking like the actors. He has identified and incorporated himself with them. The apostle Paul recommends this same mechanism for Christians only *he wants it to be consciously owned* rather than unconsciously assimilated. **Hear** him in I Cor. 3:21-23 "For all things are yours. Whether Paul, Apollos, or Cephas, all are yours. Ye are Christ's and Christ is God's" To a group of immature and jealous people the apostle divulges the secret of how to claim everything desirable in Paul, Peter, Apollos, and life in general. That secret is found in the fact that everything worthwhile belongs to God. Christ belongs to God, and we belong to Christ, therefore everything they have is ours. So why quibble about the parts when you can have the whole.

In other words, Paul was saying, "If you will but claim these men as your very own, and *as a part of you*— you can claim everything they possess. If Paul is the better preacher, then through your love, identification and incorporation, make Paul yours. If Apollos is the epitome of eloquence—claim him as your very own and you have eloquence to spare.

AN EVERY DAY EXAMPLE

Let us consider a father who was not afforded a formal academic education. In turn he compensates therefor by seeing that his son gets the very best. Then what happens? Does he become jealous and develop inferior feelings toward that son? Of course not. Hear him as he smilingly speaks of his son, claims him as his own with a pardonable pride, and is indeed happy for the opportunity to depreciate self a little and extol the son's success. He is already physically identified with the son, so he simply identifies and incorporates the son's attainments as his own and in doing so feels very well compensated indeed. *This is because he loves the son and claims him*—He emotionally feels the son as a part of himself! Hence, when we actually *see and feel* every other individual as a part of us, we will applaud their attainments and incorporate them as a part of ourselves. At the same time *we will also see every sinner as a part of ourselves being lost.* Such concepts will vaporize the superior as well as the inferior attitudes and cause loosely flung remarks about "sectarians" to cease. Instead some of these "sectarians" will be seen as part of self who are likewise struggling for greater enlightenment with honest hearts. We'll se every single boy and girl as our very own with a self projection as their parents. In other words, their errors will hurt as though our own flesh and blood committed them. Moreover, we'll pray and work for these same reasons. Finally, our hearts will be so full of real love that we'll wonder how we could have ever been so stupid in feeling inferior to or jealous of any soul. We'll then see the "superior as well as the inferior" as an expression of a part of ourselves.

Paul's argument of spiritual belonging and incorporation makes it possible for me to claim every preacher, song leader, elder, as being my very own. The writer (who can't draw a circle) has so claimed every beautiful baptistery painting he has ever seen. He does the same with sermons, preachers, and other colleagues, as well as just about everything that touches the spiritual realm. It is a very easy and economical way by which to have everything you really want. You get it all without paying —you just *claim!* At the same time you find your material wants actually decreasing.

When love and the insight therewith causes us to love and claim everyone as a part of self, inferiority feelings gradually disappear. Moreover, there are no reasons left for the development of superior attitudes. Maybe the fruits to be obtained from this concept of identification and incorporation were meant for us when Christ said, "It is the Father's good pleasure to give us the kingdom." (Luke 12:32). We hope so, because many of us have been taking it via incorporation of self with the kingdom's people for years! It is a part of God's psychotherapy for inferior feelings. Feelings that can cause jealousy, hate and resentment which in turn cause impaired physical and spiritual health.

As previously mentioned, we partially identify the sinner as a part of ourselves and therefore see a part of ourself as being lost. Apparently the Father is also willing that we appropriate and claim the best Christians and all they represent! This "spiritual gold" belongs to all of us who are willing to simply stake out our claims.

IMAGINATION—vs—WILL

The imagination plays a great part in feelings of inferiority, just as it does in the neuroses. A common axiom is stated thusly: "Where the imagination and the will are in conflict, the imagination always wins." This obviously assumes the imagination to be stronger than the will. We can perhaps illustrate the power and operation of the imagination by this example.

Let us assume that a downtown street is being oiled and paved. After the first oiling, twelve inch boards are carefully laid in the streets upon which the pedestrians can walk. Although they are quite narrow, perhaps most everyone could walk across the street upon a single board. But suppose that same board was supported fifty feet over the street—would the same people attempt to walk across on it? Not likely, because, imagination comes into play and overpowers the will. When this happens, another law known as the "law of reverse effect," comes into play. That law or rule asserts: "When a person wants to do something, yet believes he is unable—the harder he tries the more impossible it becomes."

For example, if an athlete, perhaps a high jumper or pole vaulter thinks he cannot go beyond a certain mark, the harder he tries the more difficult it becomes.

The same principles are often noted as factors in the person who feels inferior. That is, the self image is distorted, he feels he is "no good" or that others look down upon him and finally the imagination so crystallizes his concepts that often no amount of honest evaluation by others seem to alter his self image. He cannot see that *no man is inferior unless he deliberately wants to be.* God said as much when he equally rewarded the two talent man along with the five talent worker (Matt. 25). *God received honest effort or integrity of life from both and in effect said, "You are both equal by the standards of Heaven."* The only inferior person then is the one who is unwilling to present integrity of life (honest effort) at all times.

THE BIBLE—(God's Psychotherapy)

— In Illness and Suffering —

Briefly, our purpose of this chapter will be that of dignifying illness and suffering while illustrating how both may be used to make greater discoveries of God, and His meanings and purposes for life. We think it begins with our understanding and appreciating our need for:

BEING STILL

In Psalms 46:10 we read, "Be *still* and *know* that I am God. . . ." This appears so paradoxical to our equat-

81

ing learning and progress with constant movement that we find it almost impossible to be still for any reasons whatever. Yet, the divine command reads, "Be still and know!"

It will be noted that both knowledge and learning can come from our being still. Significantly, the word "still" in the quoted text comes from a word which means to literally "let go." That is, God is saying turn loose of yourself and relax. To have the time then to literally "be still" is really an opportunity and not necessarily an adversity. We can make it either—according to our reaction.

We recall a lady who suffered a fractured limb and subsequently developed a pneumonia. Her reaction was, "Why did this have to happen to me—What have I done? I'm helping others and they need me!" After, permitting her to "ballyhoo" for a while, we agreed (with tongue in cheek) that maybe God was both cruel and unfair, else her accident would have befallen the writer. Whereupon we invited her to get up from her bed and go home and let the writer occupy the bed and she could then serve him. She took the hint, after which we autographed her cast and with a wink bade her goodbye and left her to think it over. In essence, our conversation with her paraphrased some of the words of David in Psalms 4:4 "Commune with your own heart upon your bed, and *be still*." Apparently, she did a little thinking, and found time to consider the actual blessings of sickness, the services and importance of the others; along with the great interdependencies of the human race. We noted that she had gained a message of unselfishness and humility when she left the hospital. She had learned the importance of *"being still."* Perhaps this and similar cases can give

82

meaning to an even more urgent need for rest. Let us note Psalms 23:2 "He maketh me to lie down."

It appears that the statement is usually interpreted as relating to quiet, peace and plenty of green pastures. To this, we can subscribe providing we are willing to accept God's means of reaching the ends.

First, it will be noted that it reads: "He maketh me." This is not a matter of choice, it is absolutely imperative —lie down we must! Too many valuable lessons are forever missed if we never lie down, whether in sickness, prayer, the quiet hour, or in other ways. We recall the story of an Arabian shepherd which vividly illustrates our lesson.

One day the shepherd was met by a stranger who noticed him holding in his arms a sheep with a broken front leg. Noting that the shepherd seemed to be giving such tender and careful attention to the properly splinted leg; the visitor stated: "I see one of your sheep has suffered an accident and broken a leg." The shepherd smiled sympathetically and replied, "No, not an accident—I broke it!" "But why, sir?" asked the traveler. "To teach him" replied the shepherd. "You see, this sheep began to wander off by himself to seek his food and water. Sometimes others would follow. But now, he must lie down and depend upon me for his food and water. I both feed and water him three times daily. *He will now learn that he can depend upon me.* Hereafter, he'll follow me and remain in his place with the others." And so it is with each of us—lie down we must, if we are to learn the lesson of trust.

Hence, every illness presents an opportunity for more serious thinking, appreciation, gratitude and growth in power with God. As stated elsewhere, every pain can be borne with a feeling of worship to God, and for someone else who is more badly needed by others.

When Jesus counselled the disciples in regard to the destruction of Jerusalem and other problems, he ended by saying "In these establish ye your souls." In other words, find yourselves (Luke 21 chapter).

Israel of old was unable to see and appreciate the power of God at the Red Sea, until they could: "Stand still, and see the salvation of the Lord" (Exodus 14:13).

Be it remembered and pondered well, that when we are upon our bed, God is literally saying "With you too, I am risking some of my reputation in your hands during your illness and suffering—care then for it cheerfully." Moreover, "In your patience (endurance) possess ye your souls."

HE LEADETH ME

In pastures green? No always. Sometimes He
Who knoweth best, in wisdom leadeth me
In weary paths where heavy shadows be,
Out of the sunshine, warm and soft and bright,
Out of the sunshine, into darkest night.
I oft would faint with sorrow and afright
Only for this: I know He holds my hand,
So whether led in green or desert land
I trust, although I may not understand.

Beside still waters? No, not always so;
Ofttimes the heavy tempests round me blow
And o'er my soul the waves and billows go,
But when the storms beat loudest, and I cry

Aloud for help, the Master standeth by
And whispers to my soul, "Lo, it is I!"
Above the tempest wild I head him say,
"Beyond the darkness lies the perfect day,
In every path of thine I lead the way."

So, whether on the hilltop high and fair,
Or in the sunless valleys where
The shadows lie, what matter? He is there!
And more than this, where'er the pathway lead,
He gives to me, no helpless broken reed,
But His own hand, sufficient for my need.
So where He leads me, I can safely go,
And in this blest hereafter I shall know
Why in His wisdom he has led me so.

Author Unknown

HALLELUJAH!—I HAVE A THORN
(Read Cor. 12:1-10)   (Moffatt)

In the above text the apostle Paul tells of his being caught up into paradise and hearing sacred secrets which no human lips can repeat. He then states that there is really nothing to be gained by his telling or boasting of it, but inasmuch as some vain boasters seem to be degrading him, he does choose to mention it, then place it in proper perspective. He says, "My wealth of visions might have puffed me up, so I was given a thorn in the flesh, an angel of Satan to rack me and keep me from being puffed up. Three times I prayed the Lord to relieve me of it but he told me: *It is enough* for you to have my grace; it is in weakness that my power is fully felt." Thus he concluded, "I am proud to boast of all my weaknesses and thus to have the power of Christ resting

85

on my life. It makes me *content* for Christ's sake, *with* (note—with) *weakness, insults, trouble, persecution and calamity; for I am strong just when I am weak."*

— The Key —

In these statements the inspired Saint gives us the key to power, contentment, deeper insight and God-Centeredness. First off he apologizes for having to deviate from a Christ centered message to talk about visions and revelations. He wants it understood that others are *not* providing the stimuli by which his actions are determined nor his life lived. Whereas many place premiums upon "visions," with some religious movements altogether founded upon such supposedly peripheral events; Paul lets it be known once and for all that his texts for preaching and living are found elsewhere. He realized the dangers and harm of seeing behind the veil but not seeing through things. Consequently he indirectly warns us against "spiritual peeping." Perhaps most of those who dwell upon prophecy and in turn establish dates for world events have never learned Paul's lesson in this respect. They seem to think that they have "peeped" where no one else has ever seen. Some minds can only thrive on the spectacular, which certain "prophetic and healing texts" seem to fulfill for them. They have never learned to be content with the power that comes from meekness and receptivity, rather than the pseudo ego strength that one derives from ostentation.

For many, it is an unacceptable paradox that real power lies in resignation to God. We cannot seem to learn that the most powerful individual is one who has fully resigned himself to God's ways, but will never surrender to anything else. Here again is the "meek who inherits the earth"! True, the meek observes others as they "piddle" with some of it, but with God, the meek has it—all of it. Paul next proceeds to show us the "blessings of thorns in the flesh." If you have ever had either a splinter or a thorn, his figure of speech can be "keenly" appreciated! Who wants a splinter? No one solicits them, but we do get them. The apostle says that he learned how to use them.

— THE ANSWER —

First, ask God to remove them, but if not his will then accept the necessary grace to handle them—and that without grumbling. And may we suggest that they never become "useless calamity, illness nor surgery tales" for idle or unprofitable conversation. They should not be used as "organ recitals"! Actually what happens to you or the writer amounts to very little. It's what happens to others that really counts. Our *genuine* happiness depends not upon what happens to us but what we make happen to others. Now back to Paul. He sought the Lord three times to remove his thorn but the Lord had better things for him. He said, *"It is enough for you to have my grace*—it is in weakness that my power is fully felt."* (Moffatt) Paul saw it, believed and resigned himself to it, and maybe later wished he could have "bristled with thistles"—Each thistle would have simply meant more power, poise, grace, serenity and contentment.

Finally, as the good apostle grew into more spiritual insight and poise, he would seem to review the entire event (from the vision to the thorn) and wrap it up with —"Hallelujah, I'm Hindered!"

It is significant that he follows in the next chapter (13) with, "It is no weak Christ you have to do with, but a Christ of power." (vs. 3—Moffatt) Again, it is in our weakness when that power is fully felt. Only then does it fully rest upon our lives. Remember—when we have *no* hindrances and get things done, we are very likely to interpret our accomplishments as being due to our own power. But when in spite of the thorns we become conquerors, we are more likely to accept the results as having come from the Power above resting upon us. This makes us more like He who conquered with thorns to spare. Indeed a crown of them!

Chapter 6

CHURCH

— In Relation to God —

It appears that with some the church has been permitted to supersede God in the redemption of man. For example, we recall a conversation with a Roman Catholic in which he asked how people were saved before Christ came and established His church. To our Catholic friend, the absence of the church simply meant no church as a *saving institution* with all her ceremony, pomp and priesthood. To him, God was a creator who was more or less helpless, dethroned, or side-tracked until a church could be started to save the world.

Some Protestant groups have expressed the same concepts. The writer has about all of his life listened to ministers who set the church forth to the world as a great saving institution. Biblically it is neither saving, nor an institution nor is it depicted as saving anyone. It is called a body, and depicted as an organism— (not organization) —saved from sin by the Savior—Jesus Christ. God was incarnated in Christ to save the world and the revelation of this incarnation was the invasion of God into human life. Jesus therefore did not die for the right to establish an institution or organization that could save the would. He died to save the world and those who accept Him constitute the saved (from their past sins—the delivered) *and these are not the Savior,* but only the church!

It is easy to observe how an undue emphasis upon institutional salvation would de-emphasize God salvation. This unintentional de-emphasis is clearly noted by the statements so often heard as when a church member becomes dilatory or backslides. He is referred to as having become "unfaithful to the church"—not as a traitor to God, which he is. If a member is financially liberal he is referred to as being "liberal to the church"—not as a supporter of God. On and on we could go with such connotations that bespeak our thought framework and concepts.

Such teaching and preaching has in turn resulted in somewhat of a brotherhood concept of churchanity together with herd and institutional salvation rather than one of Christ emphasis and deliverance. This would in turn tend to de-emphasize the enormity of our personal guilt and sin, and minimize the grace of God whether one realizes it or not.

This unintentional de-emphasis of God and exaltation of the church results in other tragic consequences. It cheats the Christian in many ways, and can prove especially disappointing to the new babe in Christ. This results from one trying to draw and live upon institutional resources rather than Heaven's. And—there is a difference! People are sometimes left with the impression that all blessings are in the church and they believe it. Later, when the church (people) disappoints them, and they're sure to come, these disappointed believers discover themselves to have been primarily anchord to an institution (of people) rather than to the Anchor within the veil.

Our thoughts are not intended to minimize the

healing and redemptive fellowship of God's people, nor the importance of the church in relation to both sinner and God. Above all, we are not willing to leave the impression that one church is as good as another. Everyone knows that belief actually amounts to "by-lief" (what we live by) and this most certainly makes a difference. It is for this same reason that some congregations are better than others. Their fruits prove it by the irrefutable rule of Jesus: "By their fruits ye shall know them."

God, Christ and the church all have a definite Bible perspective, but this is distorted when we either create or leave the impression that the world is to come to an institution for salvation, rather than to Christ. The institutional concept tends to discourage a personal or individual salvation and substitute a group or herd deliverance. Because of this we have wondered if some haven't almost unintentionally suggested that we will be saved and lost as groups. This is akin to what sometimes appears as "flock salvation" when evidenced by people, like sheep, running up to the flock "getting dipped" (instead of meaningful baptism) with the bleat: "Here I am—I'm one of you" without a personal and wholehearted surrender to Christ. In this way they seem to think they'll be saved "when the herd (whether saints or not) goes marching in."

— Fellowship —

The most profound statement in the entire word of God relative to the meaning of fellowship is couched in these words: And He appointed twelve *to be with Him.*" (Mark 3:14 Moffatt) This meant that in spite of their sins, ignorance, pride, egotism, prejudiced religious

91

concepts, etc.; the master appointed them to be with Him. This was the first formal step taken in the beginning of the greatest fellowship movement the world will ever discuss and Heaven will ever witness. We can think of no one single act of Jesus that better illustrated the interpretation which Heaven itself gives fellowship, and which, it would seem, should be adequate for all of us who feel no holier nor wiser than Heaven! The Master herein revealed the richness, love and magnamity of His heart when he literally said "I'll accept you as you are." Truly, this was the heart of God exposed! Nothing, absolutely nothing, can stimulate more love and devotion, more willingness to learn and develop and create more awe for the good and pure; than God Himself saying. "I need you, I'll take you—I am willing to risk a portion of my reputation and program in your hands." Such is enough to literally create Heaven in the souls of twelve men or choke them to death—depending upon their gray matter!

— Bigness of Fellowship —

No one single act of Jesus more displayed His being Nothing showed his invasion into human living more than this striking and refreshing action. Conversely, nothing could have more revealed his gross spiritual immaturity and pee-wee similarity to us, than his failure to have so worked. Evidently then, the meaning of Christian fellowship is defined as *being with Jesus*. From there on, the growth and development of that fellowship depends upon our enlargement of this relationship with Him. Moreover, our being in fellowship with Him makes us in fellowship with every other person who sustains spiritual relationships with Christ—*whether we prefer it or not!*

This is because God has made it so, and it is not dependent upon our accepting or rejecting these people. Physically, we are part of every human being on earth, and we are likewise spiritually a part of every human being united to Christ. His being tied to all of us simply ties us together. We may kick and fret, disown one another, and show our infantilism by refusing to recognize one another, but the relationship is there. The quicker we learn and emotionally accept these truths—the better.

— Results of Fellowship —

Because Jesus understood and initiated the real application of fellowship, He was able to attain great results in His work. His plan worked and continues to work in proportion to His workers' concepts and expression of true fellowship. This is exactly why some people and groups go through life getting results while others only get consequences. By working in harmony with the spiritual and moral undergirding of all revealed truth as revealed by Christ, the Bible and nature, the results are attained. In other words, *understanding what the Bible means* rather than "what it says" and applying what it means, gets results. Thinking we know what it means (we are specifically referring to fellowship) but missing that meaning, causes us to get only consequences. In view of our wealth of consequences but poverty of results, it would seem that we would be ready to restudy and re-evaluate our disappointing interpretations of the word "fellowship."

— Fellowship Not To Be Equated With 100% Approval —

It is immediately evident to even the kindergarten student of the Bible that Jesus did not equate His fellowshipping the disciples and others as agreeing with, or condoning, everything they might believe and do. If He had, the same would have at once dethroned God. His accepting them to be with Him simply meant that He would take them *in spite* of what they were and not because of it. This is attested by Paul in Rom. 15:7 "Receive one another as Christ also received us. . . ." (could the thought of our condescending to others perhaps make it a little easier, or furnish the needed rationale for some of us to fellowship others?) Paul means that God condescended to accept us, rather than having us work ourselves up to Him by the ladder of knowledge, purity, accurateness, etc.; to where he would say, "Now you are what you ought to be—you know enough—I'll take you." Hence His fellowship with us is based not upon what we are, but upon what *He is.* Likewise, our fellowshipping others is not to be based upon their quality but ours. The same is true with love, is it not? Loving people, *really* loving them, reveals not what they are but what we are. This is why one's capacity for fellowship is somewhat determined by his capacity for love. Many people who profess to love simply do not know the difference between real love and domesticated hatred. Their failure to fellowship proves it. And frankly, the capacity for love is almost entirely dependent upon one's emotional maturity.

— Christ—Vs—Phariseeism —

The Pharisees, and sometimes the disciples, made the colossal blunder of thinking that God only fellowshipped people because of what they were. That is why they yelled at Christ, "This man received sinners." Their atrophied hearts could not conceive of God receiving a man who in their opinion was not what he ought to be. They couldn't see that *it is because of what God is that people are received,* rather than the worthiness of the people. As a whole, we have apparently been unable to see it any differently!

Like the disciples who told Jesus of finding those who were casting out devils and then forbidding them, we have reacted the same way toward others who are trying to cooperate with Christ in casting Satan out of the hearts of men. We too, have equated "not being with *us*" as "not being with Christ." And of course, Jesus hands us the same answer: "He that is not against us is on our side." (In other words—"Let's claim them!") Hence, we find Christ receiving and fellowshipping people whom we reject.

He never made a *perfection* of knowledge, doctrine, character, understanding and deportment the conditions of fellowship. He wanted only a perfection of love. That is, all the love the heart could muster as it grew—the rest could follow. The same should be sufficient for all of us today.

Because of our limited concepts of the meaning of the word fellowship we once again cheat ourselves. (The ignorant are always cheated.) Because we have equated fellowship and even social intercourse, with approving and condoning the religious tenets and practices of others, we have failed to utilize the opportunities to learn from them. It is true that we'll often take their books and commentaries and study them in seclusion, but we are unwilling to get such information first hand where possible.

Like our Catholic friends, we have refused to attend religious services other than our own, and in some cases we have equated doing so with eternal damnation. It would indeed be refreshing to see Christian people both *willing and unafraid* to go and sit at the feet of some of the most learned and godly people of the various Christian movements. This can be done with great profit if we can ever learn that our doing so isn't "fellowshipping error" and "bidding it God-speed." Moreover, we might learn some additional truth and inject it into our own brotherhood blood stream. This would go far toward inhibiting the religious inbreeding that has so long been among us. Heretofore, the only noticeable deviation from our incestous dogmatism has been that of some of our educators (in our own schools) who were willing to seek some light from outside sources. In our opinion, these men have perhaps saved us from total mental stagnation and spiritual myopia, plus providing some needed fresh stimuli for everyone. They have done it, and almost without exception, remained steadfast in their faith.

There is another mutual benefit that can come from religious and social intercourse with others. We find it in the common good we may accomplish in community efforts that help all. It may be attempts to eradicate gambling, liquor, vice, etc.; where all possible support is needed. When we fail, as we so often do, to join in these efforts; we appear to others as "Having a form of Godliness, but unwilling to have anything to do with *religion as a force*." (2 Tim. 3:5 Moffatt) For those who may be fearful of such community cooperation, let us hasten to add that it is not necessary for us to lose our religious identity and reasons for existence by such cooperation. We don't become sectarian by associating with "sectarians" anymore than Jesus became a sinner by associating with sinners.

Let's begin to take the lead in such noble efforts and then invite others to join us and *our platform* in accomplishing the ends.

— WORSHIP —

One of the most noticeable tragedies of many Christians is that of divorcing religion from daily life. We are not just referring to the well known practice of acting it out on Sunday and forgetting it the remainder of the week. We are speaking of Christians failing to understand that their work, recreation, and illnesses are all a part of Christian living and worship—a failure to understand that all facets of life should express worship. Only the superficial thinker can accept a religion that is unrelated to life, and the more superficial our concepts the more apparent the unrelatedness.

By holding a religion that is not wholly related to life, one can easily see how the meaning of worship would be distorted, prostituted and set aside only for special days and occasions. Such concepts have given rise to expressions like "going to worship"—"corrupting the worship" —"the divine pattern for worship," and many other similar phrases. The idea that the Christian is always in a state of worship by his thoughts, work, and play seems very remote to those who can only conceive of worship as expressed by ritual, songs, prayer, teaching, etc. They cannot see a man actually worshipping God as he gives a full day's honest work for his pay. Society and the church would today attribute these efforts to about everything under the sun except worship. Yet the thinking Christian knows full well that all of his honest efforts are in glory and praise to his Maker. (By the way, if more Christians would keep this in mind, their work would be far more pleasant. (Col. 3:17 & 23) The same is true with suffering, abuse, etc.—Jesus so taught that we do it for His namesake.) Let it be understood then that work, honest work, even slavery, can be worship to God. And what, by the way, do we suppose kept the songs alive and hearts looking upward among so many of our negroes during slavery, unless it was that they bore such bondage for God. Their religion was related to life and like Paul they could say, "May the grace of God be with you all" when we all know that they were the ones who needed it. Let us not be misunderstood as thinking that congregational worship is not vitally important, but our group services should be seen for what they really are—people with a true *condition of want,* rather than as an advertisement of sanctity. Our services are wonderful diets of worship but not the end within themselves. They are helpful means to the end.

— THE CITY WITHOUT A TEMPLE —

Strangely enough, the greatest conception of worship ever formed and conveyed to may was that of a city of people without a church or temple. John saw the Holy City without a temple, but wherein the servants saw God face to face and had His name written in their foreheads. We think it significant that John saw a city because a city would seem to depict the busy life of humanity in everyday dress. Cities have always been places of work and idleness, sickness and health, along with plenty and poverty, plus crime and sin in contrast with the lives of saints. Our interpretation of John's vision does not permit us to limit its full meaning and realization to the post-judgment. We think the vision also includes the teaching that *as man serves God, he becomes more and more the real temple in which God dwells in preference to a temple made with hands*. It will be noted that John relates that just as man served, he also saw the face of God. This is always true. No man sees more of his Maker than what he does in partnership with that Maker. The more he cooperates, the more he sees.

Note too, that God's name is written in their foreheads. The name has always indicated the character. The ancients would change the name when the character changed. (The name Joses simply means "one more." Joses's other name "Barnabas"—means "son of encouragement." There is a vast difference in being a Barnabas rather than a Joses in the kingdom of God.) These people in the city of God had the character or name of God branded (not whitewashed) upon their foreheads. This branded name meant something. All of this, but yet no temple! Why? Because this city was the truly *transformed city. It was the true expression of worship—they worshipped night and day*. Yet this worship was in the form of being devoted servants to the Most High. This gives meaning to Paul's teaching that Christians are the temple of the Holy Spirit.

— WORSHIP NOT CONFINED TO A PLACE —

One of our greatest misconceptions could be that of trying to channel and confine New Testament Christianity to a semi-sacred spot called a church building, with group activity therein called worship, and above all, wherein all work and worship would trickle down to where it runs only through an organization. Let us emphasize again, that what church services really indicate would be the *needs* and *wants* of Christians. At formal

99

services the thinking Christian drinks deeply of the food afforded (too often this is pretty thin soup) and leaves with his God both enshrined and enthroned in his own heart, and with His Majesty's name stamped in his forehead. He has the intent purpose of increasing his worship as he serves mankind and in so doing makes every person and everything he contacts a city without a literal temple.

— WORSHIP—NOT JUST CERTAIN ACTS —

Worship then is not to be viewed only as certain prescribed acts in which it finds its true and greatest expression. To largely confine the meaning of worship to acts and patterns is to cheapen it and reduce it to mere formula and ceremony. Giving such acts an improper emphasis causes some to place a premium upon protecting "the acts of worship" from corruption, innovations and additions, while leaving the *deeper meaning* of Christian worship untouched and at the "mercy" of the devil himself. Some people think the only way one could corrupt the worship would be to add to the so-called "items of public worship." They are wholly unable to see how they can corrupt their adoration and veneration of God (worship) and prostitute his temple (their lives) by plain everyday *mediocrity of life*. With many, their wanting a full day's pay for half hearted effort is not a corruption of worship—it is Bible approved "W.P.A." Consequently, more enlightened people without the church see this and choke on it. These same church people can see how Ananias and Sapphira lied and shammed, but that reason their mediocrity of effort is wholly unlike it—if they even see any comparison at all. As aforestated, too many of us can see a so-called divine pattern of worship consisting of songs, prayer, Bible teaching, communion and contributing, but are wholly unable to see the deeper divine pattern of everyday worship as demonstrated by Jesus the Christ. His was not a secular life and a worshipping life. He had but one pattern—an integrated life. He never had a mere day of worship, nor certain acts of worship. His life was the divine pattern of all worship. Let's not confuse the patterns!

Furthermore, our failure to conceive of worship as being more than just some acts performed in congregational expression has caused us to fret, frown, and fight over the wrong things. Have you ever known of brethren expending very much effort, money, and preparation in order to debate someone over things that corrupt the life pattern (worship) of the individual member as they often do in regard to various so-called doctrinal issues? Why, practically everyone knows that certain members who would "die" if a piano were introduced into the public worship would never trouble themselves about the other. Proof of this is the fact that they will attend a debate but not a prayer meeting. Nor, will they seldom make personal calls upon corrupted members. This pattern of thinking and living is rather shallow!

— GRASPING THE DOMINANT THOUGHTS —

Perhaps no one can ever know the real meaning of worship and Christianity until he grasps the dominant thoughts of Christ. The woman at the well, and other Samaritans missed the meaning of worship because they thought it involved above all else—a mountain. Mt. Gershim was that mountain upon which Abraham supposedly offered Isaac and traditionally the Samaritans venerated it. To them *the place* was all important. On the other hand the Pharisees likewise missed the deeper meaning of worship and came up with ceremony, rites, mint, cuminn and anise. Both cases show what happens when we miss the leading thoughts of Christ and his *program for life*. To miss these dominant thoughts and settle on a few proof texts of dogma that are usually wholly unrelated to life is to settle for a cheap religion that produces cheap results. Moreover, it causes us to take the paths of loneliness and unproductivity as did the aforementioned Pharisees. Such a course is spiritually lonely because no *thinking person* is going to fall in line with a group who by a *few proof texts distorts the whole program of God and in so doing makes the kingdom uninhabitable for serious and thinking people*. Needless to say, those who fail to grasp the program of Christ are as barren as the fig tree denounced by Christ and may end up in the same way.

— CHRIST CLAIMED DIVINITY VIA HIS PROGRAM —

One of Christ's claims for divinity and superiority was that of His great dominant thoughts for mankind in relation to God's program for life on this planet. He introduced, lived and taught it and in turn crumbled world empires. It is more than saddening today to see sincere but ignorant people relegating these thoughts to the background and teaching that the kingdom of God finds true expression through "meat and herbs" concepts, rather than peace and joy in the Holy Spirit. People of old took these dominant thoughts and turned the world upside down. Today, we overlook these very thoughts and instead come up with "One cup," "Scrip-

102

tural worship," "No Bible Classes," etc.; then trot off to church, eat the communion, "burp,"—return home to sit down to a big meal and turn only our dinner plates right side up and think we too are shaking the world! Again, we fail to see that the farther we are from the core of things, the closer we are to the marginals. For this reason we frequently major in both minors and marginals! It is past time that we restudy these points and aim at the "bulls-eye." A starting place might be found in understanding that God is as equally interested in the purity and integrity of our private worship (life in all facets) as He is in the public convocation. We'll show that we are beginning to grasp the core of these things when we become more Christ-centered with lives that tally with Godliness.

IDENTIFYING
THE CHURCH

Elsewhere, we make the assertion that more unity exists among us than we are recognizing and enjoying. This is based upon our personal belief that those who constitute the church are joined together and united in a very special way, and therefore create a special type of unity. The apostle Paul uses the human body to illustrate this very point. (Rom. 12) He points out that while all members are not alike and do not perform alike, they are nevertheless members of the same body and indeed very important members at that. Some of these members may be frail, emaciated or even paralyzed, but they are nonetheless members of that body to which they are attached. Certain physical handicaps may preclude a much desired unity of expression, cooperation and function, but it would be silly to assert that a fractured or even paralyzed arm is not a part of the body. Paul nails it with these words, "For as the body is *one* and hath many members, and all the members of that one body being many *are one* body—*so also is Christ.*" (1 Cor. 12:12). In view of this divine illustration, it is evident that all of us, regardless of our brotherhood segment, our relative ignorance, our faults and short-comings are members of Christ's body. All of us who have been born again (John 3) have been enrolled in Heaven and are brethren under our Father. To deny this would be as ridiculous as denying that we are not re-lated to our own blood brothers and sisters. And just here, permit us to add that we should treat one another as we would our own flesh and blood (assuming we are cultured to begin with). It makes no difference as to whether we use "one cup or a thousand"—"cooperate or don't cooperate"—"oppose our colleges or support them from the church treasury"—"eat in our church buildings or on the parking lot"; we are all brothers in Christ because Heaven has tied us together through the new birth. We can fight, fuss, fume and feud all we please, but this does not "unborn us" nor sever the spiritual tie. We are yet brethren in *Him!* Such differences can never destroy that deeper union and unity that exists, but only blur and distort the expression of it. Our blundering and perhaps shameful treatment of one an-other can of course hinder the body's growth, cause it much pain and hinder its effectiveness, but we cannot destroy its *real unity.* Nor are we overlooking the fact that some of us could be eternally lost for knowingly mutilating the body and insulting our Lord, but we are just as quick to assert that the many sincere saints who have been zealous, honest and active in their mistaken views and concepts, present an altogether different picture. We personally cannot feel that any of our brethren have actually intended to harm or hinder the cause of Christ. We *err* when we do not regard our sincere honestly mistaken brethren as being a part of and as representing the true church. We must learn that sincere differences, thinking "out loud" and growth are not necessarily to be equated with catastrophe. For too long we have seemed to regard "everything old as sacred and everything new as wrong." We *must not* regard brethren who honestly cannot see "eye to eye" with us as being false teachers, heretics and dangerous. Above all, we must not accuse them of wilful wrong. This can largely be avoided if we will not force certain consequences and conclusions upon those who have not honestly reached them. Also, we suspect a lot of brethren would, like Zacchaeus, come down out of the tree, if we would cease our barking and help them to descend both graciously and gracefully. Instead, we have heretofore waited until a brother was "forced" out on a limb, and then we sawed the limb off and thought we had helped preserve the purity of the church. Has it never occurred to us that when a brother goes too far out on such a limb that our common decency and Christian culture should cause us to want to help him if necessary, to save face and further embarrassment. Would we appreciate a school teacher attempting to make a fool out of one of our children because the child was honestly mistaken? Would we appreciate the child's being "written up" in the school paper and embarrassed before all? Yet it appears that in the past we have occasionally stooped to such levels. In such heated controversy we have even made statements to the effect that the other party "knows better." Here, we carelessly pose as mind-readers with suprnatural power, while stamping modern faith healers as fakes and frauds for claiming that same power.

WHICH GROUP AMONG US IS THE TRUE CHURCH?

Many times we have heard it carelessly flung, that certain congregations and segments are not the *"true* church—they are not the *loyal* church." May we now ask just which segment among us is the "loyal one"? In order to answer this, we must first answer: "loyal to what?" Every single segment among us has its own unwritten creed, party loyalties, traditions, cliches, shibboleths, badges, standards and tests of doctrinal purity. How then are we going to determine loyalty? Reader, don't reply—"By God's word of course"—because that is exactly what each segment among us has parroted for years. All of us think we are speaking as the Bible speaks. In fact, some of us seem to be *"infallibly"* sure of it and wonder why all others cannot see "things that are so plain." So to simply say, "let us just agree on the Bible" is to greatly oversimplify the matter. *This type of agreeing hasn't been seen (in the manner we desire) since the Bible was written.* This is largely because we have not recognized our natural brotherhood strata of differences in human thought and comprehension, along with the many, many factors that influence our interpretations and practices. Instead we have for years taken our misused, misunderstood and worn out slogans and under the illusion of preserving truth and the church, created segment after segment and then preserved them with our high and impregnable walls of disfellowship. Of course this was a natural consequence that was certain to follow our conclusions that the New Testament church was fully restored. Believing that everything has been finalized has in turn resulted in our taking our so-called doctrinal points and "acts of worships" (about five) together with a meeting house with a rather exclusive use of "Church of Christ" over the door and stamping ourselves as the true church—the one body, if you please! Not only have we claimed to be the IT—BUT THE ALL OF THE IT!

Believing that we have all the truth (doctrinally or externally) would naturally result in our opposition to anything new. Having these externals (often with the soul untouched) made us feel that to learn, or add anything, was to attempt to improve upon that which was already complete. ("Ye are complete in Him"— Col. 2:10—has been a forbidding proof text.) For example, those in the past who have vigorously opposed written human creeds and "uninspired literature" had this "profound" and quick answer. "If it's more than the Bible, it's too much. If it's less than the Bible, it's too little. And, if it's just like the Bible, we don't need it." Of course, we overlooked our own bed-sheet charts and blackboard outlines. Wonder why? Simply because we haven't *fully* understood what we have been saying all through the years.

After having settled upon our previous conclusions with reference to doctrine and practice (but with much unrecognized tradition) we were necessarily forced into our next reactionary step. This was to take a "firm stand" in order to prevent digression, going beyond, drifting, adding to and perverting the "true gospel." Text after text was developed to warn us of the disaster that could follow our accepting anything new or untried.

107

This again produced more "paralysis by analysis." The disease and its syndrome is yet among us. A part of which is seen in our confusing principles with methods, organism with organization, and in our eternally probing in efforts to come up with patterns, examples and inferences for everything we do and say. At the same time we have well succeeded in rearing up from within us a rather large group of legalists, Pharisees, and Bible technicians. A by-product of all of this has been our "famous" chapter and verse, proof-text and straw-man debating type of sermons which we have often confused with preaching. We apparently have not stopped to realize that we can teach a parrot to do the same thing. With these sermons have come lessons upon lessons focusing such examples as Uzziah touching the ark, Moses smiting the rock, and Noah with the gopher wood as warnings to those who are not "one hundred percenters." These and similar scriptures have frequently been distorted and overworked, but have served to ever warn us of what we *think* James said in the following words: "For whosoever shall keep the whole law and yet offend in one point, is guilty of all." (Jas. 2:10) Our erroneous concept of "one hundred per cent-ism" has of course influenced us in regarding everyone else in the brotherhood as not being the "true church" and has also produced some soul-quakes among us at the same time. We have reasoned that we had "just as well miss it a mile as to miss it an inch." Likely too, we have overplayed our serving with "fear and trembling."

Being sincere in these concepts and interpreting almost everything new as a threat to our security, caused us to next take a firm stand against "false teachers and those who would lead the church astray." This has meant that there must always be a continual purging in order to keep the church (our segment) pure and loyal. The sectarians and heretics must be kept out. As always, we must have authority for what we practice, so we naturally went to such scriptures at 2 John 9-11 "Whosoever transgresseth and abideth not in the doctrine of Christ hath not God. He that abideth in the doctrine of Christ hath both the Father and the Son. If there come any unto you and bring not this doctrine, receive him not, neither bid him God speed. For he that biddeth him God Speed is a partaker of his evil deeds." Of course "this doctrine" was always equated with both our personal and our segment concepts. Consequently, to have anything to do with a brother who didn't agree, meant that we were partakers of his evil deeds. It apparently never dawned upon us that neither Christ nor the apostles ever once practiced our distorted concepts of these verses. Along with this we found the same inspired John telling us that the only way we could have fellowship with God (and of course with one another) was by walking "in the light." The catch was, we usually equated "walking in the light" with "walking by our own lanterns." These same warped concepts are yet being taught and practiced. But alas, John further enhanced and potentiated our interpretations by adding "And hereby we know Him if we keep His commandments. He that saith I know Him and keepeth not His commandments is a *liar* and the truth is not in him." (1 John 2:3) Now that settled it! Here was Bible authority for actually calling a liar any brother who disagreed with our doctrine. In fact we felt that we were actually using "God's personal branding iron." We didn't have to brand them as "liars and false teachers"—we *would let the word of God* do

109

it, we reasoned. And, if this one couldn't fit, we went to Mark 16:17 . . . "Mark them that cause divisions and offences contrary to the doctrine which ye have learned and avoid them." This we have done to the extent that we almost expect others to stand afar off and cry unclean, unclean, unclean!" But just in case we felt the danger to be an emergency, Titus 3:10 furnished authority for quick amputation: "A man that is a heritic after the first and second admonition reject." If necessary we could admonish him in both the morning and afternoon of the same day and then reject him. (A sort of count down type of discipline before we placed him into Satan's orbit.) And, of course, heresy in all Christendom has always meant just one thing—"a false teaching"—something different from the written or un-written creed. Purging the "heretics" has always been a must in order for God to have anything to do with those of us who remained pure. After all hath he not said, "Wherefore come out from among them and be ye separate, said the Lord and touch not the unclean thing, and I will receive you." (2 Cor. 6:17) (Our history proves that we have emphasized the "be ye separate"). Hath He not also told us, "Have no fellowship with the unfruitful works of darkness but rather reprove them." (Eph. 5:11) These and other similar scriptures have furnished the needed authority for the continual slicing and whacking by brethren at brethren. While we have likely conceived of ourselves as always perform-ing some very important and God-authorized surgery in order to preserve the church from "ravaging doctrinal cancer" we have instead been making a cadaverous dis-section of the body of Jesus Christ. The further shame and disgrace of this ignorance has been supplemented by

110

the various "party surgeons" taking a leg, arm or foot
and then running off to their group and proclaiming:
LOOK!—We have the *true* body, indeed *all* of it! This
could perhaps be amusing if it were not so tragically true.

HOW ABOUT THIS?

Do we not have among us enough *really big* men
(the E. W. McMillan quality) who could come together
and objectively and unemotionally study our brotherhood differences in behalf of all? Could not this be
done without propositions to haggle over (as in debates)
and in a much less emotionalized atmosphere? Could
they not say: "We are here to study and discuss everything together with dignity, and in poise and prayer?
We can each follow wherever truth seems to lead, yet
with the full assurance that we can graciously retract any
statements, change our positions or views, and do anything else that is in keeping with common sense and
spirituality and feel at ease." It is our opinion that if
more of these types of meetings were enjoyed, we could
manage to shed ourselves of much of our public debating
(which too often is characterized by actual giggling and
applause) and the ever strained highly emotional content.
Perhaps these types of meetings would be another step
in genuine spiritual bigness and maturity, and in turn
also condition us for better and more effective dealings
with

"OUR OTHER BRETHREN"

It may come as a shock to some, perhaps not, for us
to assert that we believe that God has children in what
we call the denominational world. Here are our reasons
for making that assertion. We believe that whenever we

111

are born into the kingdom or family of God via the new birth (John 3) we then and there become members of God's family. We may later become disobedient, dilatory, negligent, and even cease to attend church, but we are yet members of the family of God. We would of course be considered unfaithful or back-sliding members, but members nonetheless. We can never become "unborn" out of the family which we were born into. Only at the last day will we be severed from God's kingdom and banished forever. We believe Jesus teaches this lesson as recorded in the words: "He will gather *out of* His kingdom all things that offend and them which do iniquity and cast them into a furnace of fire. . . ." (Matt. 13 Ch) If our reasoning is correct then all who are born into the kingdom will remain until the last day at which time they will be totally disinherited.

Now if it be that unfaithful and other disobedient children are yet within the confines of Christ's kingdom, how much more so with regard to those brethren who are humbly striving to walk daily with the Master but who may hold some intellectual error? Brethren whose souls and hearts are in tune with Heaven, but who unfortunately have a conceptual string or two out of tune. We believe this principle is abundantly set forth in the New Testament writings to perhaps almost all congregations. Various New Testament congregations were in error, and some of it was more serious than what exists among us today, yet these congregations were addressed as brethren and saints and fellowshipped by both the apostles and Heaven. Being steeped in Judaism didn't preclude the Jerusalem congregation as being a part of the "one body" nor can some of our intellectual errors (doctrinal errors we call them) sever us from it.

But just here perhaps someone is ready to proclaim, "Yes, I can see how brethren who were "with us" and left could perhaps be considered as erring or straying brethren, but what about those who have been immersed by preachers other than of the Church of Christ? Perhaps a reader would ask the author if he accepts "Christian Church baptism?" Our answer is that we accept Christ's baptism and reject both Christian Church and Church of Christ baptism, if there be such. The administrator has nothing whatsoever to do with whether or not one's baptism is valid. It is wholly between the candidate and his God. Our ceremonially verbalizing "I baptize you for the remission of your sins" is no more *binding* than if we attempt to *loose* by saying I baptize you NOT for the remission of sins. Our adding the *"for* remission of sins" to our ceremony can but likely, at most, satisfy the Pharisees in our audience and further enhance our unwritten creed. Moreover, if it has come to the point where we can validate or invalidate one's baptism by what we say or do not say, then I must confess that the Church of Christ has not only stolen "Peter's keys from the Catholics"—but changed the lock as well. The idea that in order to be scripturally baptized one must have it performed by a Church of Christ preacher is nothing less than reaction (likely to Baptists), tradition and pure Church of Christ-ism. But to reply more forthrightly to the last question, we would unhesitatingly say that those baptized in the instrument segment of the brotherhood are just as scripturally baptized as it is possible to be. The validity of one's baptism must be decided upon an individual basis and not by herd concept.

This being true, it is past time that we begin to recognize the instrument segment of our brotherhood as

113

brethren and above all, work toward a greater unity with them. When we have re-established our fellowship with these, we shall then be in a better position to start seeking out our more scattered brethren (born again—John 3) whose identity has become "lost in Babylon." We can then give real meaning to God's plea to them: "Come out of her My people. . . ." (Rev. 18:5) In this way, we may again uncover

— The Real Message of the So-Called
Restoration Movement —

We make no pretense of historical proficiency, but what we have read convinced us long ago that in our eagerness, we hurriedly labeled a restoration and reformation—*a complete restoration*. If Alexander Campbell wrote what occupied his mind, then his Lunenburg Letters along with other writings will show that he was trying to gather God's people from all the sects. In our opinion, here is where we have prostituted the so-called restoration movement. We have conceived of Campbell and others as having *restored the church*, while they conceived of themselves as simply restoring certain emphases and a genuine unity, while also bringing the authority of God's word into a sharper focus. Campbell was ever aware of his relationship to the historical thread of continuity of the church, but it appears that we conceive of the "restorers" as having believed there was no church of God on earth for eighteen hundred years and that their job was to find the lost seed of the kingdom and plant it again. This concept we believe to be fallacious, and a denial of plain factual history written by our own brotherhood hands. We must face up to the fact that our historical thread does not extend to Pentecost, except as

114

it finds its way through other movements, which like our own, were likely called forth to correct and improve conditions, build upon *"old truth,"* and any "new truth" that could be discovered. I realize this will remove our "halo," but it might make the angels sing in behalf of plain honesty and objectivity. If we can but recapture the *spirit* of the so-called restoration movement and profit by their mistakes we can then with our additional knowledge go forth into the world once again as in apostolic days, and cause people to see New Testament Christianity as *the* religion really worth having.

— UNITY —

Let our first statement be that we do not presume to have the answer, but perhaps some approaches that might help us toward further progress. This subject, along with many others, has been greatly over-simplified as evidenced by our attempts toward solutions and answers by formula and slogans. For example, such quips as "let the Bible be the guide" and even our usage and connotations of the more familiar one "speak where the Bible speaks and remain silent where it is silent" all show that many of us regard the attainment of unity as a rather simple procedure. These slogans and formulas all sound pretty good, but our social memory (we call it history) has proved their application to be very difficult, if not altogether impossible. Our study then will not be along these familiar lines.

To begin with, we are of the firm opinion that we are enjoying much more, yea far more unity than apparently most of us recognize. We believe this for the simple reason that recognition itself is a vital ingredient of unity, and consequently a shortage here would at once distort our perspective. This writer finds it impossible to altogether agree with the picture of disunity so often painted as existing among us. This is because we feel that *the most important ingredient of unity actually exists among us in abundance.* We refer to the *unity of purpose* which we believe to have been uppermost in the mind of our Lord when he prayed the words recorded in John 17. In *purpose*—we believe the church has always been united else it could never have crumbled world empires and convinced the world of Christ's invasion of our planet. If it has not been united, then we will have to admit that the "stone cut out of the mountain" without hands (the church) has done her job while torn asunder by division. This we cannot conceive. Her victorious triumphs have been made in spite of the fact that the *type of unity of which the brotherhood largely conceives* has never existed in any century—not even the first! It appears then that we are definitely united in the same manner and to the same extent as has always been the case; namely, in *unity of purpose.* This view seems to be enhanced in view of the greater efforts and continuity of purpose which has characterized us since World War Two. While we, no doubt, have much farther to go and much more to accomplish, the results abundantly show that we are GOING. Being united in this great purpose of saving man is what both Heaven and mankind desires, with perhaps the observation that our "argumentation among good people in the meantime is but more knowledge in the making." It must be remembered that the early congregations had their troubles and differences, yet there was a unity of purpose that prevailed and could not be destroyed. The New Testament epistles occasionally bristle with corrective measures for many of these congregations, yet no writer seemed to even dream of the "unity picture" being as badly distorted as we often paint it. Their fellowship was maintained, their love cords remained intact and never once has the writer found even a suggestion or hint that those brethren gave recognition to the rather shallow differences that seem to often arrest our attention. In fact the *only* point of "doctrinal differences" which we can find that was to be made a test of fellowship was the Deity of Christ. II John vs:11 deals with those deceivers who were teaching that Christ had not come in the flesh. The brethren were therefore warned and told that "if any come unto you and bring *not* this doctrine (that Christ has come in the flesh) receive him not into your house, neither bid him God speed." Today we take this out of context and use it as a justifiable reason for excluding everyone from our fellowship who does not see practically everything as we do. The term "this doctrine" is usually equated with our own particular brand of the various offerings of "Church of Christ-ism." It can mean one cup, long hair, short hair, our concepts of modest apparel, no Bible classes, etc. If the writer's concepts of unity are anywhere near truth, then the chief sin and problem of the Church of Christ is not disunity but sectarianism. We know that many will literally howl at this, but we also happen to know that those who will likely howl the loudest are those who are either wholly ignorant of the term "sectarian" or blind as bats—maybe both! If these words seem to be caustic and unnecessary, we humbly add that they are simply made to perhaps cause some of our readers to thoroughly study the meaning of the term for *perhaps* the *first* time. For example, if the reader believes that the word has to do wholly with the belief and teachings

117

of a false doctrine—he is a mile away. Just here we are led to further show that unity of purpose means that

UNITY IS NOT UNIFORMITY

It appears that many of us have thought that if we all did things in the same way, adapted the same protocols and procedures; we would have unity. In other words, if we *appeared alike*—we would be alike. Nothing could be farther from the real meaning of unity; and the greatest proof of it is the awesome expression of oneness in our universe—"THE UNITY OF NATURE." It proves that UNITY CANNOT BE IDEALLY HAD AND EXPRESSED WITHOUT DIVERSITY! This is the only way to avoid blanket uniformity, which we repeat, so many are equating with unity. If this unity with diversity concept can be both intellectually and emotionally accepted, it will bring us much further along our way. We inject the word "emotionally" because history and present communication among us testify that we have largely thought our differences to be almost altogether doctrinal in origin. We are now finally realizing that psychological, sociological and economic barriers are indeed very important factors. We have learned that our beliefs not only represent our faith but our *measurement* of thought as well. Similarly, our "conclusions of truth" accurately record and express exactly those measurements we were willing to settle for at our various ages and periods of study and growth. Thus, with some newer measurements and perhaps keener insights among us, it seems that some of our brethren are now being sincerely applauded for "thinking out loud." This is both healthy as well as a very good sign of better things to come. Our only word of admonition or suggestion might be that we be ever mindful of the twilight deception of easy relativism as a possible reaction to our former smugness of absolutism.

PATTERNS AND PREMISES

In dealing with unity versus uniformity it is interesting to try and ascertain certain factors that have contributed to our confusion of the terms. We feel that much of this has been derived from our concepts of the above sub-heading. For example, we have for years been taught that the church is the only *organization* by which, in which, and through which our Bible teaching, benevolent work and similar responsibilities are to be carried out. During these many years, it apparently has seldom dawned upon us that we may have misinterpreted and misapplied our main proof text—*that we may have assumed our premise!* We have not seen that while we were quoting Eph. 3:21 "Unto Him be all glory in the church" that what we were actually believing and saying would appear in print like this: ". . . Unto Him be all glory in the church *organization*" (elders, deacons, etc.). In other words, we have not recognized that "Unto Him be all glory in the church" is *not* the same as "Unto Him be all glory in the church *organization*." This is bound to be true for the simple reason that the church can exist without what we conceive as constituting its organization. For example, if a man and his wife are the only Christians on the remotest island—they are the church. No super-structure of what we call "an organization" is necessary before they can be Biblically identified as the church on the isle of Peace. Would not every thing they did in Jesus Name glorify that name? And after all, isn't this exactly what counts? But here we have hit another snag. We so often hear the remark "the church is to get the glory!" Well, who said so? Who concocted the idea that we "sinful" and unprofitable servants are to get any glory for anything? This type of phraseology bespeaks our eternally thinking of the church as an *institution* to gloat over. The author somewhere got the idea that the church is to glorify Christ, instead of attempting to glorify ourselves. The scripture reads ". . . *Unto Him be glory* in the church (in us) by Jesus Christ. . . ." (Eph. 3:21) We have perverted it to read: ". . . *Unto the church be glory"* with Christ and God as mere onlookers.

Now religious organizations (which are actually organized methods) are not simply wrong because they are organizations doing these good works. The missionary society is not wrong because it is an organization. (Organization per se simply is not wrong.) It is wrong because of the control it exercises over congregations. It is the abuse committed that can make our own organizations wrong. Religious papers are organizations doing a good work (most of the time) and would only become wrong or sinful by what they do, or when they abuse their rights to exist. The same may be said for our Christian schools and similar efforts. What we must see and understand is that our schools for example, are not just supplements to the home, private enterprises, etc. *They are organizations approved of God which give genuine meaning and expression to the church of the living God via Christians at work in every sphere, facet and domain of human life*. Every thinking person knows full well that it is *purely Christian purpose and devotion* which is the undergirding and causal factors of all these fine efforts. As a result of that purpose and devotion, our Lord Jesus Christ is being glorified in this manner. *This too, is the church at work.* Away with our apologetic approach that schools mainly exist to secularly educate our children, but where the Bible is only taught—"incidentally." Hogwash! Take the Bible teaching and training out of them and what would soon happen to their influence upon the impressionable souls who attend? We insist that all such efforts including youth camps, orphan homes, eleemosynary foundations, and similar efforts are *all a credit and glory to God;* and are a direct result as well as *an expression of the church in action.* Once again, we say—away with this concept that all the good work for God has to be channeled through the "oversight of a local organization" which too often could not *"sightover"* the work (spiritual myopia) much less oversee it. Let us now turn to

PATTERNS

We have long been taught and trained to look and ask for patterns. Sometimes the author wonders if we haven't almost developed "pattern obsessions." It seems that when good brethren begin some good work, the first thing we hear is "Where is the pattern?" Most of us think there must be one or else we cannot proceed. Because of this, we have no doubt carved out a few where there really weren't any. We have taken simple narratives and just plain necessary communication and thought we saw "patterns of operation in them."

The brother who holds for only one cup simply reads, "And He took the cup" and retorts "there it is in black and white." He does this as though Christ died so he could demonstrate the use of "one cup" for humanity.

The brother on the next rung of the ladder who, for example, insists on laying his money on the table simply turns to Acts 4:35 and reads, "And laid them down at the apostles feet." In his case the pattern does not include the feet—only laying it down. (Tradition of course of the deepest dye)

The next brother who is on rung three of exegesis is amused at these "technicalities" as he likely names them, but is sure he sees a pattern in I Cor. 16:2 "Upon the first day of the week let each of you lay by in store. . . ." Consequently, he feels that the first day of the week is the only day upon which a contribution may be publically taken. Yet he may be the very one who makes the announcement in which members are requested to bring at the next mid-week service some food for the so-called "food barrel," kitchen or emergency stock—just in case of a fire, etc. Now just what do these "scholars" think these gifts constitute?

On the next rung we have those who go along with the procedure just mentioned but would never (Heaven forbid) pass a collection plate to the congregation at a mid-week service. That too, might violate the pattern or be interpreted as "drifting." So instead, they just apologetically stand the missionaries or orphan home representatives at the door and *Pass The Congregation By Them*." If the thoughtful reader should pursue it, it is most likely that he could continue going right on up our ladders of similar interpretations and applications.

Because of our looking too persistently for "patterns" we have definitely discouraged Christian spontaneity. This in turn dampens faith, zeal and unusual service. Consequently, "few alabaster boxes are being broken" (a spontaneity of devotion by which Jesus was deeply touched) nor are "men being carried and let down through the roofs" into the presence of Christ. Our established patterns and conventionalities have made us believe that such cases must always be channeled through the doors.

It would appear that many of our so-called approved patterns are nothing short of *our own approved customs and traditions*. For example, where would one turn in the New Testament to find a pattern for congregational singing? We accept it as being both good and profitable, but where is the pattern? Frankly, it is not to be found! Instead, we could in our opinion come closer to finding one for a solo. (I Cor. 14:26) The context shows that Paul was correcting some abuses in the public congregational worship. He did not condemn one's chanting or singing of psalms—he only regulated it along with speaking in tongues, revelations, etc. As he said, "Let all things be done unto edifying." Would we be willing to permit a dear brother to sing a solo in our services today? The writer would, and for several reasons.

When a boy. he observed an elderly saint (an elder) do this rather often. We recall Bro. John C. Wise occasionally breaking forth in song at the Lord's table or maybe while giving an exhortation to the flock. His sincere devotion, along with a long white beard created within us an image of Moses or Elijah. Often his songs would have to end as he choked back his tears. We are told that Bro. Flavil Hall and perhaps other saints often interrupted their sermons to give special meaning to both their lesson and the song with a *sincere* solo. Brethren, was this wrong? God forbid! But someone may say, "Oh, that's different!" Yes, and in what way is there a difference? Could not the same be done today if we could scrape up the same brand of saints?

The problem is, we have stifled or maybe killed the spontaneity that always openly or latently accompanies genuine spirituality. We have so strongly reacted to "what denominations have done" that we quite often fail to make our own decisions and act in view of our own needs and considerations—*we just react!* As a result, some of us go through life with "three cheers for nothing" and "three sneers at everything." Once again, because we have seen no pattern for such spiritual manifestation as just mentioned, we have automatically relegated such opportunities for spiritual feasts to the category of "show and display." And once again, the superficial have gotten cheated.

The absence of these feasts along with some sincere "Amens" reminds us of what is said to have happened years ago in a fashionable church in Washington, D.C. A southern gentleman who thought the preacher was fervently preaching the word, climaxed a point with "Praise the Lord." Whereupon an usher tip-toed over and whispered in his ear, "Sir, you can't praise the Lord here!" Has the same happened among us with regard to "Amens"—individual and group singing? Singing mind you which could thrill our souls and *really* teach and admonish? Are we too stereotyped and afraid to do that which could sometimes serve to bring us closer to Heaven? Are we afraid of what other congregations and the brotherhood might think? Are we afraid of being "branded"? On the other hand, are those who might not be impressed or helped by these sincere manifestations willing to love, fellowship and tolerate those who are? Or would this also precipitate needless warrings and separations?

AN ANALYSIS

We believe the words of John 17:22 to hold the *key* to the unity for which our Lord prayed. "And the *glory* which thou gavest me I have given them; that they may be one, even as we are one." These words seem to place an entirely different slant upon *how* unity is to be attained and enjoyed. They seem to make it appear as the *result of something given to us* rather than a result of what we are able to devise and then agree upon. Note the words: "I have *given them, that they might be one.*"

Next, consider what must have been meant by the words, "Even as we are one." All surely recognize that we frail human beings can never be one in every sense in which the Father and Son are one. We can never have the same *degree* of unity nor the enjoyment thereof for the simple reason that we can never enjoy the same degree of power, decision, comprehension of thought, unlimited or infallible grasp of truth, etc. We can only have the same *kind!* Consequently, the words "even as we are one' must be understood in a relative or limited sense. They must be understood and interpreted in a manner that depicts our being united in some particular expression, in some unique way, as was exactly the Father and the Son. Now the only conceivable manner or degree in which we can see human beings, Christians if you please, approximating even a facet of the "Father and Son unity"—is by or in *the unity of purpose!* That unity of purpose is expressed and enjoyed in *the redemption of man!* This is precisely the work referred to in John 17:4 "I have glorified Thee on earth, I have finished the *wor*k thou gavest me to do." Now lay these phrases side by side and note that we can prac-

125

tically equate them: "The *glory* that gavest me—the *work* thou gavest me." The glory and the work are inseparable. Here then is our common unity as enjoyed by The Father and the Son, and in this brethren—WE ARE ONE! For this reason I've previously stated that *we are far more united than we are divided.* Let's *recognize* it!

Chapter 8

THE CHURCH— (Lunenburg Letters)

After the author had completely finished this book he recalled a conversation of a few years ago in which a brother enquired if we had read the replies of Alexander Campbell to a sister who had asked Bro. Campbell to explain his views concerning "Christians among the sects." Having been appraised in the conversation of some of Bro. Campbell's views, we managed to borrow a copy of Millenial Harbinger of 1837 and read for the first time what apparently has been captioned the "Lunenburg Correspondence." We freely admit its special import and significance for us at this time and have therefore included these significant letters for the reader's evaluation.

Several things arrested our attention. First, the courage of our Bro. Campbell in stating his convictions and "rebukes" as he called them, even though he knew such would be quite unpopular with many of his sincere and devoted brethren. Secondly, we carefully noted both the views and approach of this capable restorer and reformer with reference to those who were highly regarded as sectarian by his brethren. To us, this offers sharp insight as to why Campbell and others were highly successful in their efforts to restore more New Testament Christianity. If we mistake not, they definitely felt a pity and a compassion for those whom they regarded as "Biblically underprivileged." No superior attitudes nor spiritual snobbery ever seemed to characterize them as they ever diligently and lovingly sought to show others the "way of the Lord more perfectly." Finally, we once again see what is evidenced throughout practically all restoration writings and interpersonal relationships; namely, that of free discussion without the breaking of fellowship. The letters follow for your evaluation.

M.F.C.

LUNENBURG CORRESPONDENCE
By A. Campbell

ANY CHRISTIANS AMONG PROTESTANT PARTIES

"Lunenburg, July 8th, 1837.

"Dear brother Campbell—I was much surprised today, while reading the Harbinger, to see that you recognize the Protestant parties as Christian. You say, you "find in all Protestant parties Christians."

"Dear brother, my surprize and ardent desire to do what is right, prompts me to write to you at this time. I fell well assured, from the estimate you place on the female character, that you will attend to my feeble questions in search of knowledge.

"Will you be so good as to let me know how any one becomes a Christian? What act of yours gave you the name of Christian? At what time had Paul the name of Christ called on him? At what time did Cornelius have Christ named on him? Is it not through this name we obtain eternal life? Does the name of Christ or Christian belong to any but those who believe the gospel, repent, and are buried by baptism into the death of Christ?"

In reply to this conscientious sister, I observe, that if there be no Christians in the Protestant sects, there are certainly none among the Romanists, none among the Jews, Turks, Pagans; and therefore no Christians in the world except ourselves, or such of us as keep, or strive to keep, all the commandments of Jesus. Therefore, for many centuries there has been no church of Christ, no Christians in the world; and the promises concerning the everlasting kingdom of Messiah have failed, and the gates of hell have prevailed against his church! This cannot be; and therefore there are Christians among the sects.

But who is a Christian? I answer, Everyone that believes in his heart the Jesus of Nazareth is the Messiah, the Son of God; repents of his sins, and obeys him in all things according to his measure of knowledge of his will. A perfect man in Christ, or a perfect Christian, is one thing; and "a babe in Christ," a stripling in the faith, or an imperfect Christian, is another. The New Testament recognizes both the perfect man and the imperfect man in Christ. The former, indeed, implies the latter. Paul commands the imperfect Christians to "be perfect," (2 Cor. iii. 11) and says he wishes the perfection of Christians. "And this also we wish" for you saints in Corinth, "even your perfection:" and again he says, "We speak wisdom among the perfect," (1 Cor. ii. 6) and he commands them to be "perfect in understanding," (1 Cor. xiv. 20) and in many other places implies or speaks the same things. Now there is perfection of will, of temper, and of behavior. There is a perfect state and a perfect character. And hence it is possible for Christians to be imperfect in some respects without an absolute forfeiture

129

of the Christian state and character. Paul speaks of "carnal" Christians, of "weak" and "strong" Christians; and the Lord Jesus admits that some of the good and honest-hearted bring forth only thirty fold, while others bring forth sixty, and some a hundred fold increase of the fruits of righteousness.

But everyone is wont to condemn others in that in which he is more intelligent than they; while, on the other hand, he is condemmed for his Pharisaism or his immodesty and rash judgment of others, by those that excell in the things in which he is deficient. I cannot, therefore, make any one duty the standard of Christian state or character, not even immersion in the name of the Father, of the Son, and the Holy Spirit, and in my heart regard all that have been sprinkled in infancy without their own knowledge and consent, as aliens from Christ and the well grounded hope of heaven. "Salvation was of the Jews," acknowledged the Messiah; and yet he said of a foreigner, and alien from the commonwealth of Israel, a Syro-Phenician, "I have not found so great faith—no, not in Israel."

Should I find a Pedobaptist more intelligent in the Christian Scriptures, fore spiritually-minded and more devoted to the Lord than a Baptist, or one immersed on a profession of the ancient faith, I could not hesitate a moment in giving the preference of my heart to him that loveth most. Did I act otherwise, I would be a pure sectarian, a Pharisee among Christians. Still unless I could prove that all who neglect the positive institutions of Christ and have substituted for them something else of human authority, do it knowingly, or, if not knowingly, are voluntarily ignorant of what is written, I could not,

I dare not say that their mistakes are such as unchristian-ize all their professions.

True, indeed, that it is always a misfortune to be ignorant of any thing in the Bible, and very generally it is criminal. But how many are there who cannot read; and of those who can read, how many are so deficient in education; and of those educated, how many are ruled by the authority of those whom they regard as superiors in knowledge and piety, that they never can escape out of the dust and smoke of their own chimney, where they happened to be born and educated! These all suffer many privations and many perplexities, from which the more intelligent are exempt.

The preachers of "essentials," as well as the preachers of "nonessentials," frequently err. The essentialist may disparge the heart, while the Nonessentialist despises the institution. The latter makes void the institutions of Heaven while the former appreciates not the mental bias on which God looketh most. My correspondent may belong to a class who think that we detract from the authority and value of an institution the moment we admit the bare possibility of any one being saved without it. But we choose rather to associate with those who think that they do not undervalue either seeing or hearing, by affirming that neither of them, nor both of them together, are essential to life. I would not sell one of my eyes for all the gold on earth; yet I could live without it. There is no occasion, then, for making immersion, on a profession of the faith, absolutely essential to a Christian—though it may be greatly essential to his sanctification and comfort. My right hand and my right eye are greatly essential to my usefulness and happiness, but not to my life; and as I could not be a perfect man without them, so I cannot be a perfect Christian without a right understanding and a cordial reception of immersion in its true and scriptural meaning and design. But he that thence I will be asked, How do I know that any one loves my Master but by his obedience to his commandments? I answer, in no other way. But mark, I do not substitute obedience to one commandment, for universal or even for general obedience. And should I see a sectarian Baptist or a Pedobaptist more spiritually-minded, more generally conformed to the requisitions of the Messiah, than one who precisely asquieseces with me in the theory or practice of immersion as I teach, doubtless the former rather than the latter, would have my cordial approbation and love as a Christian. So I judge, and so I feel. It is the image of Christ the Christian looks for and loves; and this does not consist in being exact in a few items, but in general devotion to the whole truth as far as known.

With me mistakes of the understanding and errors of the affections are not to be confounded. They are distant as the poles. An angel may mistake the meaning of a commandment, but he will obey it in the sense in which he understands it. John Bunyan and John Newton were very different persons, and had very different views of baptism, and of some other things; yet they were both disposed to obey, and to the extent of their knowledge did obey the Lord in every thing.

There are mistakes with, and without depravity. There are wilful errors which all the world must condemn, and unavoidable mistakes which every one will pity. The Apostles mistook the Saviour when he said concerning John, "What if I will that John tarry till I come;" but the Jews perverted his words when they alleged that Abraham had died, in proof that he spake falsely when he said, "If a man keep my word he shall never see death."

Many a good men has been mistaken. Mistakes are to be regarded as culpable and as declarative of a corrupt heart only when the proceed from a wilful neglect of the means of knowing what is commanded. Ignorance is always a crime when it is voluntary; and innocent when it is involuntary. Now, infers that none are Christians but the immersed, as greatly errs as he who affirms that none are alive but those of clear and full vision.

I do not formally answer all the queries proposed, knowing the one point to which they all aim. To that point only I direct these remarks. And while I would un-hesitatingly say, that I think that every man who despises any ordinance of Christ, or who is willingly ignorant of it, cannot be a Christian; still I should sin against my own convictions, should I teach any one to think that if he mistook the meaning of any institution, while in his soul he desired to know the whole will of God, he must perish forever. But to conclude for the present—he that claims for himself a license to neglect the least of all the commandments of Jesus, because it is possible for some to be saved, who, through insuperable ignorance or involuntary mistake, do neglect or transgress it; or he that willfully neglects to ascertain the will of the Lord to the whole extent of his means and opportunities, because some who are defective in that knowledge may be Christians, is not possessed of the Spirit of Christ, and cannot be registered among the Lord's people. So I reason; and I think in so reasoning I am sustained by all the Prophets and apostles of both Testaments.

End of A. Campbell's first letter

133

CHRISTIANS AMONG THE SECTS (2nd writing)
By A. Campbell

In an article on a query from Lunenburg, which appeared in the September number, certain sentences have been objected to by some two or three intelligent and much esteemed correspondents. We gave it as our opinion that there were Christians among the Protestant sects; an opinion, indeed, which we have always expressed when called upon. If I mistake not, it is distinctly avowed in our first Extra on Remission; yet it is now supposed by these brethren that I have conceded a point of which I have hitherto been tenacious, and that I have misapplied certain portions of scripture in supporting said opinion. In the article alluded to, we have said that we "cannot make any one duty the standard of Christian state or character, not even Christian immersion," etc. Again, we have said that "there is no occasion for making immersion on a profession of the faith absolutely essential to a Christian, though it may be greatly essential to his sanctification and comfort." These two sentences contain the pith and marrow of the objectionable portion of said article, to which we again refer the reader.

Much depends upon the known temper and views of a querist in shaping an answer to his questions. This was the case in this instance. We apprehended that the propounder of the queries that called for these remarks, was rather an ultraist on the subject of Christian baptism; so far at least as not to allow that the name Christian is at all applicable to one unimmersed, or even to one immersed, without the true intent and meaning of baptism in his understanding pervious to his burial in water. This we gathered from her epistle; and of course gave as bold an answer as we ever gave—perhaps more bold than on

134

any former occasion, yet nothing differing from our former expressed views on that subject.

My high regard for these correspondents, however, calls for a few remarks on those sentences, as farther explanatory of our views. We cheerfully agree with them, as well as with our sister of Lunenburg, that the term Christian was given to them because they were immersed, but because they had put on Christ; and therefore we presume to opine, that, like every other word in universal language, even this term may be used as Paul sometimes uses the words saint and sinner, Jew and Gentile—in a part of their signification.

We have, in Paul's style, the inward and the outward Jews, and may we not have the inward and the outward Christians? For true it is, that he is not always a Christian who is one outwardly: and one of my correspondents will say, 'Neither is he a Christian who is one inwardly.' But all agree that he is, in the full sense of the word, a Christian who is one inwardly and outwardly.

As the same Apostle reasons on circumcision, so we would reason on baptism:—"Circumcision," says the learned Apostle, "is not that which is outward in the flesh;" that is, as we apprehend the Apostle, it is not that which outward in the flesh; but "circumcision is that of the heart, in the spirit, and not in the letter (only,) whose praise is of God, and not of man." So is baptism. It is not outward in the flesh only, but in the spirit also. We argue for the outward and the inward—the outward for men, including ourselves—the inward for God; but both the outward and the inward for the praise both of God and of men.

Now the nice point of opinion on which some brethren differ, in this: Can a person who simply, not perversely, mistakes the outward baptism, have the inward? We all agree that he who wilfully or negligently perverts the outward, cannot have the inward. But can he who, through a simple mistake, involving no perversity of mind, has misapprehended the outward baptism, yet submitting to it according to his view of it, have the inward baptism which changes his state and has praise of God, though not of all men is the precise question. To which I answer, that, in my opinion, it is possible. Farther than this I do not affirm.

My reasons for this opinion are various; two of which we have only time and space to offer at this time. Of seven difficulties it is the least; two of these seven, which, on a contrary hypothesis would occur, are insuperable:— The promises concerning an everlasting Christian church have failed; and then it would follow that not a few of the brightest names on earth of the last three hundred years should have to be regarded as subjects of the kingdom of Satan! !

None of our brethren regard baptism as only outward. They all believe that in the outward submersion of the body in the water, there is at the same time the inward submersion of the mind and heart into Christ. They do moreover suppose that the former may be without the latter. They have only to add that it is possible for the latter to be not without the former in some sense, but without it is the sense which Christ ordained.

Still my opinion is no rule of action to my brethren, nor would I offer it unsolicited to any man. But while we inculate faith, repentance, and baptism upon all, as essential to their constitutional citizenship in the Messiah's kingdom, and to their sanctificationa and comfort as Christians, no person has a right to demand our opinions on all the differences of this generation except for his private gratification. He is certainly safer who obeys from the heart "that mould of doctrine" delivered to us by the Apostles; and he only has praise of God and man, and of himself as a Christian, who believes, repents, is baptized, and keeps all the ordinances, positive and moral, as delivered to us by the holy Apostles.

The scriptures quoted in the essay complained of, are all applied to the Christian character, and not to the Christian state, as contemplated by one of our correspondents. They are therefore not misapplied. It is hoped these general remarks will be satisfactory on this point. A.C. Ohio River, Sept. 28th, 1937.

ANY CHRISTIANS AMONG THE SECTS?
(3rd writing)
By A. Campbell

Judging from numerous letters received at this office, my reply to the sister from Lunenburg has given some pain to our brethren, and some pleasure to our sectarian friends. The builders up of the parties tauntingly say to our brethren, "Then we are as safe as you," and "You are coming over to us, having now conceded the greatest of all points—viz. that immersion is not essential to a Christian." Some of our brethren seem to think that we have neutralized much that has been said on the importance of baptism for remission, and disarmed them of much of their artillery against the ignorance, error, and indifference of the times upon the whole subject of Christian duty and Christian privilege.

My views of Opinionism forbid me to dogmatize or to labor to establish my own opinion, and therefore I hope to be excused for not publishing a hundred letters for and against said opinion. Only one point of importance would be gained by publishing such a correspondence: and I almost regret that we have not a column to spare for it. It would indeed fully open the eyes of the community to the fact that there are but few "Campbellites" in the country. Too many of my correspondents, however, seem to me to have written rather to show that they are not "Campbellites," than to show that my opinion is false and unfounded.

While, then, I have no wish to dogmatize, and feel no obligation to contend for the opinion itself, I judge myself in duty bound to attempt—

1st. To defend myself from the charge of inconsistency.

2nd. To defend the opinion from the sectarian application of it.

3rd. To offer some reasons for delivering such an opinion at this time.

I. With all despatch, then, I hasten to show that I have neither conceded nor surrendered any thing for which I ever contended; but that, on the contrary, the opinion now expressed, whether true or false, is one that I have always avowed.*

1. Let me ask, in the first place, what could mean all that we have written upon the union of Christians on apostolic grounds, had we taught that all Christians in the world were already united in our own community?

2. And in the second place, why should we so often have quoted and applied to apostate Christendom what

---

* It is with us as old as baptism for the remission of sins, and this is at least as old as the "Christian Baptist." Read the first two numbers of that work.

the Spirit saith to saints in Babylon—"Come out of her, my people, that you partake not of her sins, and that you receive not of her plagues"—had we imagined that the Lord had no people beyond the pale of our communion!

3. But let him that yet doubts, read the following messages from the Christian Baptist, April, 1825—"I have no idea of seeing, nor wish to see, the sects unite in one grand army. This would be dangerous to our liberties and laws. For this the Saviour did not pray. It is only the disciples dispersed among them that reason and benevolence would call out of them," &c.&c. This looks very like our present opinion of Christians among the sects ! ! ! 2nd ed. Bethany, p. 85.

4. Again, speaking of purity of speech in order to the union of Christians, we say, "None of you (Christions) have ever yet attempted to show how Christians can be united on your principles. You have often showed how they may be divided, and how each party may hold its own; but while you pray for the visible unity of the disciples, and advocate their visible disunity, we cannot understand you." March, 1827, vol. 4.

5. Various essays and letters on "Christian union" from our correspondents, are given to our readers with our approbation; from one of which we quote these words:—"I suppose all agree that among Christians of every name there are disciples of Jesus Christ, accepted of God in him, real members of his body, branches in the true vine, and therefore all one in Christ." October, 1826, vol. 4, p. 53.

6. In a letter to Spencer Clack, August, 1826, I have said "As to what you say concerning the evils of division among Christians, I have nothing to object. I sincerely deplore every division, and every sectarian feel-

ing which now exists; and if I thought there was any man on this continent who would go farther than I to heal all divisions and to unite all Christians on constitutional grounds, I would travel on foot a hundred miles to see him and confess my faults to him" vol. 5, p. 15.

7. On the evening before my departure to debate with Mr. Owen, vol 6, p. 239, April 6, 1829, in alluding to that crisis, I say—"I rejoice to know and feel that I have the good wishes, the prayers, and the hopes of myriads of Christians in all denominations." So speak the pages of the Christian Baptist on many occasions.*

8. The views of the Millennial Harbinger on this subject are condensed in a work called "Christianity Restored," or as we have designated it, "A Connected View of the Principles," &c. "of the Foundation on which all Christians may form one communion." (See its title page! !)

9. In that volume there is a long article on the foundation of Christian union, showing how the Christians among the sects may be united. We refer to the whole of this article from page 11 to 128, as the most unequivocal proof of our views of Christians among the sects. Indeed we say (page 102) of our own community, that it is a nucleus around which may one day congregate all the children of God. In that article we wax bolder and bolder, and ask, (page 121,) "Will sects ever cease? Will a time ever come when all disciples will unite under one Lord, in one faith, in one immersion? Will di-

---

* Let the curious reader consult the essay on Christian Union in the Christian Baptist, so far as I have approbated them, especially my replies to an Independent Baptist.

140

visions ever be healed? Will strife ever cease among the saints on earth?"

10. But in the last place, in the first Extra on Baptism for Remission of Sins, we exclude from the pale of Christianity of the Pedobaptists none but such of them as "wilfully neglect this salvation, and who having the opportunity to be immersed for the remission of sins, wilfully neglect or refuse"—"of such" indeed, but of none others, we say, "We have as little hope for them as they have for all who refuse salvation on their own terms of the gospel." 1st Extra, 1st ed. p. 53.

With these ten evidences or arguments, I now put it to the candor of those who accuse us of inconsistency or change of views, whether they have not most evidently misrepresented us. Were it necessary we could easily swell these ten into a hundred.

II. We shall now attempt to defend this opinion from the sectarian application of it:—

1. It affords them too much joy for the consolation which it brings; because it imparts no certainty of pardon or salvation to any particular unbaptized person whatsoever.

In reference to this opinion, all the unimmersed are to be ranged in two classes; those who neither know nor care for this opinion, and those who know it and rejoice in it. It will require but a moment's reflection to perceive that those who care nothing for this opinion will not rejoice in nor abuse it; and that those who would, for their own sake, rejoice in it are not included in it. He that rejoices in such an opinion, for his own sake, has had the subject under consideration; and it is a thousand chances to one that he is obstinately or willingly in error on the subject; and, therefore, in the very terms of the opinion, he is precluded from any interest in it. His joy, indeed, is strong presumptive evidence against him; because it is proof that he is one-sided in his feelings, which no upright mind can be—at least such a mind as is contemplated in the opinion; for it respects only those who have, without any examination or leaning, supposed themselves to have been baptized.

In no case, indeed, can there be the same certainty (all things else being equal) that he who was sprinkled, poured, or immersed on some other person's faith; or that he who was sprinkled or poured on his own faith, shall be saved, as there is that he that first believes and is then, on his own confession, immersed, shall be saved. In the former case, at best, we have only the fallible inference or opinion of man; while in the latter we have the sure and unerring promise of our Saviour and Judge. It cannot be too emphatically stated that he that rejoices for his own sake, that he may be accepted by the Lord on his infant or adult pouring, or sprinkling, because of his dislike to, or prejudice against believer's immersion, gives unequivocal evidence of the want of that state of mind which is contemplated in the opinion expressed; and has proved himself to be a seeker of his own will and pleasure, rather than rejoicing in the will and pleasure of God; and for such persons we can have no favorable opinion.

2. But that the aforesaid opinion does not disarm us of our arguments against ignorance, error, and indifference, is evident; because it assumes that the person in question is acting up to the full measure of his knowledge upon the subject, and that he has not been negligent, according to his opportunities, to ascertain the will of his Master; for in the very terms of the opinion he is not

justified, but self-condemned, who only doubts, or is not fully persuaded that his baptism is apostolic and divine.

3. To admit that there may be Christians among the sects, does not derogate from the value or importance of baptism for the remission of sins, any more than it derogates from the superior value and excellency of the Christian Institution to admit that salvation was possible to the Jews and Patriarchs without the knowledge and experience of all the developments of the New Testament. For besides the Christian disposition, state, and character, there are the Christian privileges. Now, in our judgment, there is not on earth a person who can have as full an assurance of justification or of remission of sins, as the person who has believed, confessed his faith, and been intelligently buried and raised with the Lord; and therefore the present salvation never can be so fully enjoyed, all things else being equal, by the unimmersed as by the immersed.

4. Again, as every sect agrees, that a person immersed on a confession of his faith is truly baptized, and only a part of Christendom admits the possibility of any other action as baptism: for the sake of union among Christians, it may be easily shown to be the duty of all believers to be immersed, if for no other reason than that of honoring the divine institution and opening a way for the union and co-operation of all Christians. Besides, immersion gives a constitutional right of citizenship in the universal kingdom of Jesus; whereas with our opponents, themselves being judges, their "baptism" gives the rights of citizenship only in some provinces of that kingdom. For as far as baptism is concerned, the Greek, the Roman, the English, the Lutheran, the Calvinian, the Arminian, the Baptist communities will receive the

immersed; while only a part of Christendom will acknowledge the sprinkled or the poured. Therefore, our opinion militates not against the value of baptism in any sense.

5. In the last place, to be satisfied with anything that will just do in religion, is neither the Christian disposition nor character; and not to desire to know and do the whole will of God, places the individual out of the latitude and longitude of the opinion which we have advanced. These things being so, then we ask, wherein does the avowal of such an opinion disarm us of arguments for professor or profane, on the value of the baptism in the Christian Institution; or the importance and necessity of separating one's self from all that will not keep the commandments of Jesus; and of submitting without delay to the requisitions of the illustrious Prophet whom the Almighty Father has commanded all men to obey?

III. In the third and last place, we offer some reasons for delivering such an opinion at this time:—

1. We were solicited by a sister to explain a saying quoted from the current volume of this work, concerning finding "Christians in all Protestant parties." She proposed a list of questions, involving, as she supposed, either insuperable difficulties or strong objections to that saying; and because she well knew what answers I would have given to all her queries, I answered them not: but attended to the difficulty which I imagined she felt in the aforesaid saying.

2. But we had still more urgent reasons than the difficulties of this sister to express such an opinion:—Some of our brethren were too much addicted to denouncing the sects and representing them en masse as wholly aliens

from the possibility of salvation—as wholly antichristian and corrupt. Now as the Lord says of Babylon, "Come out of her, my people," I felt constrained to rebuke them over the shoulders of this inquisitive lady. These very zealous brethren gave countenance to the popular clamor that we make baptism a saviour, or a passport to heaven, disparaging all the private and social virtues of the professing public. Now as they were propounding opinions to others, I intended to bring them to the proper medium by propounding an opinion to them in terms as strong and as pungent as their own.

The case is this: When I see a person who would die for Christ; whose brotherly kindness, sympathy, and active benevolence know no bounds but his circumstances; whose seat in the Christian assembly is never empty; whose inward piety and devotion are attested by punctual obedience to every known duty; whose family is educated in the fear of the Lord; whose constant companion is the Bible: I say, when I see such a one ranked amongst heathen men and publicans, because he never happened to inquire, but always took it for granted that he had been scripturally baptized; and that, too, by one greatly destitute of all these public and private virtues, whose chief or exclusive recommendation is that he has been immersed, and that he holds a scriptural theory of the gospel: I feel no disposition to flatter such a one; but rather to disabuse him of his error. And while I would not lead the most excellent professor in any sect to disparge the least of all the commandments of Jesus, I would say to my immersed brother as Paul said to his Jewish brother who gloried in a system which he did not adorn: "Sir, will not his uncircumcision, or unbaptism, be counted to him for baptism? and will he not condemn you, who, though having the literal and true baptism, yet dost transgress or neglect the statutes of your King?"

3. We have a third reason: We have been always accused of aspiring to build up and head a party, while in truth we have always been forced to occupy the ground on which we now stand. I have for one or two years past labored to annul this impression, which I know is more secretly and generally bandied about than one in a hundred of our brethren may suspect. On this account I consented the more readily to defend Protestantism; and I have, in ways more than I shall now state, endeavored to show the Protestant public that it is with the greatest reluctance we are compelled to stand aloof from them—that they are the cause of this great "schism," as they call it, and not we.

Now, with this exposition in mind, let us examine the meaning of the alleged concession. And first let me ask, What could induce us to make it at this crisis? Or, I should more correctly say, to repeat it so strongly?

No one will say our opponents have compelled us by force of argument to make it. Themselves being judges, we have lost nothing in argument. All agree that the "concession" was uncalled for—a perfect free-will offering.

Neither can they say that we envy their standing, or would wish to occupy their ground; because, to say nothing of our having the pure original gospel institutions among us, regarding us merely as a new sect like themselves, we have no reason to wish to be with them, inasmuch as we have the best proselyting system in Christendom. Faith, repentance, and baptism for the remission of sins, with all the promises of the Christian adoption and the heavenly calling to those who thus put on

146

Christ, is incomparably in advance of the sectarian altar and the straw—the mourning bench, the anxious seat, and all the other paraphernalia of modern proselytism. That it is so practically, as well as theoretically, appears from the fact of its unprecedented advances upon the most discerning and devout portions of the Protestant parties. No existing party in this or the father-lands has so steadily and rapidly advanced as that now advocating the religion of the New Testament. It has been successfully plead within a few years in almost every state and territory in this great confederacy, and even in foreign countries.

All agree, for a thousand experiments prove it, that all that is wanting is a competent number of intelligent and consistent proclaimers, to its general, if not universal triumph, over all opposing systems. We have lost much, indeed by the folly, hypocrisy, and wickedness of many pretenders, and by the imprudence and precipitancy of some good brethren: yet from year to year it bears up and advances with increasing prosperity, as the present season very satisfactorilly attests.

Do we, then, seek to make and lead a large exclusive sect or party? Have we not the means! Why then concede anything—even the bare possibility of salvation in any other party, if actuated by such freshly and selfish considerations? With all these facts and reasonings fresh in our view, I ask, Is not such a concession—such a free-will offering, at such a time, the most satisfactory and unanswerable refutation that could be given to the calumny that we seek the glory of building a new sect in religion? If, then, as some of our opponents say, we have made a new and an unexpected concession in their favor, we have done it at such a time, in such circumstances,

147

and with such prospects before us, as ought (we think) henceforth to silence their imputations and reproaches on the ground of selfish or partizan views and feelings.

Some of our fellow-laborers seem to forget that approaches are more in the spirit and style of the Saviour, than reproaches. We have proved to our entire satisfaction, that having obtained a favorable hearing, a conciliatory, meek, and benevolent attitude is not only the most comely and Christian-like, but the most successful. Many of the protestant teachers and their communities are much better disposed to us than formerly; and I calculate the day is not far distant when many of them will unite with us. They must certainly come over to us whenever they come to the Bible alone. Baptists and Pedobaptists ar daily feeling more and more the need to reform, and our views are certainly imbuing the public more and more every year.

But to conclude, our brethren of Eastern Virginia have been the occasion at least of eliciting at this time so strong an expression of our opinion; and we have now many letters from that region for one from any other quarter on the aforesaid opinion. Had not some of them greatly and unreasonably abuse the sects, or countenanced, aided, and abetted them that did so, and had not a few in some other regions made Christianity to turn more upon immersion than upon universal holiness, in all probability I would have answered the sister from Lunenburg in the following manner and style:—

The name Christian is now current in four significations:—

1. The ancient primitive and apostolic import simply indicates follower of Christ. With a strict regard to its original and scriptural meaning, my favorite and

oft-repeated definition is, A Christian is one that habitually believes all that Christ says, and habitually does all that he bids him.

2. But its national and very popular sense implies no more than a professor of Christianity. Thus we have the Christian nations, as well as the Pagan and Mohometan nations; the Christian sects as well as the sects political and philosophical.

3. But as soon as controversies arose about the ways and means of putting on Christ or of making a profession of his religion, in a new and special or appropriated sense, "a Christian" means one who first believes that Jesus is the Christ, repents of his sins, is then immersed on confession into Christ's death, and thenceforth continues in the Christian Faith and practice.

4. But there yet remains the sense in which I used the term in the obnoxious phrase first quoted by our sister in Lunenburg. As in the judgment of many, some make the profession right and live wrong; while others make the profession wrong, but live right; so they have adopted this style—"I don't know what he believes, nor how he was baptized, but I know he is a Christian." Thus Adam Clarke quotes some poet—

> "You different sects who all declare,
> "Lo! Christ is here, and Christ is there!
> "Your stronger proofs divinely give,
> "And show me where the Christians live!"

Now is this acceptation of the word, I think there are many, in most Protestant parties, whose errors and mistakes I hope the Lord will forgive; and although they should not enter into all the blessings of the kingdom on earth, I do fondly expect they may participate in the resurrection of the just.

The words Jew, Israel, Circumcision, disciple, are used in the same manner, even in the sacred writings: "They are not all Israel that are of Israel"—"An Israelite indeed"—"The true circumcision"—"A Jew inwardly and outwardly"—"Then are you my disciples indeed," &c.

I am glad to see our brethren so jealous of a correct style—so discriminating, and so independent. They are fast advancing to the habit of calling Bible things by Bible names. They only misunderstood me as using the term in its strictest biblical import, while in the case before us I used it in its best modern acceptation.

I could as easily at first as at last have given this reply to our sister's queries; but I thought the times required something else—and I was not mistaken. I have no doubt but it will yet appear to all that I have pursued in this the more useful and salutary course.

Our Eastern brethren were indeed, I opine, hasty and precipitate enough in expressing themselves—almost indeed before they had time to hear and consider the whole matter. I wish they had been as prompt on another occasion, and I should not have been addressed on this subject by the worthy sister so often named. But we are all learning and progressing towards perfection. If any of them, and not all, wish their communications to appear in this work, accompanied with a few pertinent remarks, I am in duty bound, according to my plan, to publish some of them.

I do not indeed blame them altogether for being prompt; for I had rather be an hour too soon as half an hour too late; yet I think some resolutions which I have received, were, upon the whole, rather premature. May the Lord bless all the holy brethren, and give them understanding in all things! A.C.

— Additional Comment by M.F.C. —

We do not wish to convey by our incorporation of these letters that we agree with Bro. Campbell in every conclusion and explanation. We do feel however, that his views will serve notice that some of this author's are not necessarily new to brotherhood concepts.

We also feel they convey another "slant" on the point we endeavor to emphasize in the following chapter. That is, responsibility with reference to certain teachings, may not actually be reached until we are in various favorable stages of life or maybe never.

Above all, may they serve to give us better insight in our attempts to help those whom the Lord urges "Come out of her MY people." (Rev. 18:5)

THE CHURCH

— Covenant Relationship —

Perhaps most of us will agree that a child is born in a spiritually safe condition. It is also our opinion that most of us feel that this security is enjoyed until the age of accountability is attained. Of course, this age or time is relative, and no one knows just when it is reached. As far as we know no one attempts to judge that chronological factor.

Let us think of a child born into an ideal Christian home where he will receive the best possible training in the Lord. He will grow up in prayer, Bible study, church attendance, and all conceivable Christian training and environment. As each year passes, his faith is deepened and his trust evidenced. Now may we ask just when will the lad lose his spiritual security with God and need baptism? Assuming of course that he prayerfully continues the same pattern of life day after day, week after week, and year after year? *When is it that his prayers for forgiveness will go unheeded (maybe without his knowing) and his need for baptism become imperative?*

—— Age Factors ——

Would it be safe to say that the boy is safe *until he realizes his need* for immersion and *REALLY BELIEVES HE WOULD BE LOST WITHOUT IT?* May we also inquire if the boy himself is to make the baptismal decision or should others try to make it for him? Should he do it of his own choosing and without coercion in any way?

Let us consider some of the factors that will influence this lad in making some of his decisions. It will be understood that he has a chronological, mental and emotional age. He may be fifteen chronologically, nineteen mentally, and nine emotionally. How will these factors influence his study, thinking and the conceptions formed? What about the psychological, sociological and broad environmental stimuli to which he has been subjected through no choice of his own? Also, will most of us be able to take into consideration some possible predisposing hereditary factors unrecognized by us but known to God. For example, understanding the part our emotional needs play in our interpreting truth and reality, could his emotions be affected by his mother having suffered from a rather severe endocrine disorder? We think so and definitely feel that there is just too much involved in the determining of one's responsibilities to God, for you and the writer to judge. For example, to which of these previously mentioned ages does God attach the most importance and/or responsibility? (Keep in mind that practically all of us can accept certain truth intellectually before we can emotionally. If this were not true the greater portion of psychotherapy would be a snap.) Does not the Omniscient One weigh all of these, and no doubt scores of other factors, in determining guilt and responsibility? To the learned reader these questions are not hypothetical, but have to do with the facts of everyday reality. What we are suggesting is that *the chronological age may be a comparatively small factor in determining guilt and responsibility* in relation to the teachings of God. We believe that most people recognize this *principle* for the simple reason that no one would think of an imbecile or even a low grade moron as being responsible before God—regardless of age.

— Emotional Arrestment —

Now the catch is, we fail to understand that *in every one of us,* various parts of the emotional life are often arrested. The psychotherapist sees this from day to day. He often sees some forty year old adult with a keen intellect dealing with some problems as would an eight or ten year old. Such a patient soon learns that he can only successfully deal with these problems when his emotional life is reopened and the development processes continued. After this he is in a position to cope with his problems and perhaps solve them after a mature fashion. All of this is similarly true in the spiritual counterpart.

We have previously mentioned in another chapter the ever present blind spots in intellectual and emotional development. Let us add, that without doubt, these various emotional arrestments in development will most certainly create certain intellectual blind spots toward certain religious truths, and also potentiate those already present. For example, let a sincere person equate the acceptance of certain religious truth with rejecting or condemning his mother and such a blind spot is evidenced. Try as hard and as long as you will, such a person will probably only accept such truth when he can harmonize it with his love and belief concerning his mother. This is an example that many will quickly recognize, but there are others which present far greater complications.

Now getting back to the boy under consideration, we are able to see a little of what makes him believe as he does and why he was molded as he was. It will be noted then that just as this sincere boy may grow up and reach the so-called age of accountability with reference to baptism wherein *he intellectually sees the need for it, sincerely feels the guilt of sin without it,* and *humbly desires to obey God in it;* we are also able to understand that another boy in an *equally* devoted family of another religious faith *may easily grow on into manhood* without ever intellectually seeing his need for it. And he most certainly will never *feel any responsibility* with reference to that which he does not comprehend. *DO YOU??* What we all need to better understand *is why* sincere people sometimes simply do not comprehend. It is quite serious to accuse people of moral dishonesty simply because they do not see things as we do.

— ACCOUNTABILITY —

What many of us fail to see is that this so-called matter of accountability is indeed a relative thing. Depending upon the rearing, environment, and "brain-washing" of the individual, one might grow up and never reach a point of accountability relative to baptism and some other teachings as we view them. His covenant relationship from the *earliest* is based upon God's grace and love anyhow (else our children are lost) and God isn't going to suddenly denounce an earnest seeker and devoted follower, who each passing day is following all the light he possesses. (Or is it likely that God does actually denounce a person at a certain age? If so, when?) It is hoped that fairness and justice will show that just as God sustains a covenant relationship with our children while they grow up and learn, so will he with *"adult children" as they continue to grow and learn. Opportunities* and *capabilities* are yet the determining factors in responsibility or else the parable of the talents of Matthew, chapter 25, means nothing in this respect. It will be remembered, that the parable shows that one's responsibilities are determined by his capabilities, willingness to cooperate, opportunities, etc.

Just here someone is ready to quip, "Well, they have the Bible and can read it—it's there in black and white!" This is weaker than pond water. The point is, in view of past training and all other factors, what will this sincere and seeking soul spiritually see when he reads the Bible? "But," adds a legalist, "If he is really seeking it he will find it. If he is honest he'll get it." HOGWASH! Are the only sincere and honest folk to be found in a movement whose people have a rash of such idiotic logic and refer to themselves as "the one body?" Was Martin Luther or John (burned to the stake) Huss sincere?

In some of our rather prejudiced thinking we can readily understand how God can love and sustain a spiritual relationship to children (as they grow up), but we cannot for the sake of us see how he can have anything to do with others who are equally sincere, devoted, sacrificial; and who honestly demonstrate the fruits of the Spirit, but *who are yet also "children"* (in respect to certain truths) in comparison to our more accurate concepts of them. Frankly they are, "Biblically underprivileged" folk who, due to various factors, have never been able to see some things which to some of us are "as clear as day."

Now, every man is expected to study, receive and obey the will of his Maker as best we can, but no individual, unless claiming infallibility (or maybe stupidity) would attempt to ascertain other people's spiritual relationship to God while those people are *earnestly doing their best to find their way* toward further growth in the Master. "Who art thou that judgest another man's servant?" To his own master he standeth or falleth." (Romans 14:4)

Perhaps if we can understand *and admit* that it is, after all, the teaching, training and many other factors that establish our own children as being accountable before God, surely, common sense and fairness would demand that the *unintentional absence of this same teaching, training and environment;* etc. would similarly evidence the lack of some responsibility and guilt. This would hold true with both our children and some adults in relation to the same commands of God. In other words, if our own children are not responsible (with reference to these teachings) *until they see and understand them; why would any other equally sincere person be—regardless of age?* Again, we say, *THE CHRONOLOGICAL AGE OF A PERSON IS BY NO MEANS THE DE-*

156

*TERMINING FACTOR OF RESPONSIBILITY TO-
WORD GOD! If it were, a forty-year-old moron would
burn in hell!*

Our presentation of these thoughts is but for one
main purpose—a better understanding of other sincere
people, together with a showing of tolerance, and flexibility of approach in our relationships and dealings with
those who disagree with us. If we operate upon the theory
that most people are wilfully blind and ignorant, we
are simply blinder than we think they are. If, however,
we can see many others as equally sincere souls who are
yet religiously under-privileged and who unfortunately
have not been exposed to certain truths nor taught
them as we; then we, like Priscilla and Aquilla, can give
meaning to the principle of love via "The way of the
Lord more perfectly." In doing so, we will come closer
to attaining the desired results.

Chapter 10

CONVERSION

Christian conversion is the *beginning of the redemption of human life from the perversion and prostitution of its God intended purposes.* It is the realignment of life to the will of Heaven, and begins when we take Jesus Christ as our personal Saviour and cooperate with His invasion into our lives. It ends only at death. This means, then, that conversion is not simply an event, but a continual process in our spiritual living and maintenance.

For too long, many have viewed New Testament conversion as being a few steps expressed by intellectual faith, (mental assent) along with repentance, confession and baptism; with baptism as the consummating act. It is true that this emphasis and arrangement does help explain the spiritual birth, but to limit conversion to this explanation is like limiting life to birth itself. Life formally begins at birth but it is not intended to end there. Hence, the exhortation of Peter to "grow in the grace and knowledge of the Lord Jesus Christ"—(I Pet. 3:18) is really an exhortation for continual conversion. Paul expresses it this way: "But we all mirror (reflect) the glory of the Lord with face unveiled, and so we *are being transformed into the same likeness as himself, passing from one glory to another*—for this comes of the Lord the Spirit (2 Cor. 3:18) — (Moffatt) Note that this transformation is in the *present tense* and expresses the *passing from one glory to another*. Obviously unless these transformations are always taking place, there can be no continual conversion! And resultingly any other so-called conversion will always end in arrestment or spiritual abortion. We believe that it was upon these grounds that Christ exhorted Peter "When thou art converted, strengthen the brethren." (Luke 22:32) We would understand this to mean that only as Peter was progressively and continually converted would he be capable of strengthening others. All Bible students know that Peter had intellectually accepted the Lord but that was about the extent. He had it "in the top of his head" but not in the "bottom of his soul." His impetuous nature and drives had to be converted and subdued. This brings us to the question of just what all is subject to conversion?

— Recognizing our Two Minds —

As noted elsewhere, man has both a conscious and an unconscious mind. We think the apostle Paul corroborates this in Rom. 7:18 through 25: "I cannot understand my own actions; I do not act as I desire to act. On the contrary, I do that I detest . . ." (Moffatt). The apostle says that this battle, is due to his inner self being in conflict with the law of his members. That is, the fleshly versus the spiritual man. In the next chapter,

159

verse 7, he states: "For the interests of the flesh are hostile to God, etc." These interests of the flesh include the natural drives of man (the ids) that have been potentiated and distorted as a result of man's depraved nature. (Note—we say distorted, because they are God given and may be properly used). These distorted interests would indeed try to make the spiritual man a "prisoner to sin's law that resides in our members." (Rom. 7:23—Moffatt). He went on to say "I serve the law of God with *my mind,* but *with my flesh* I serve the law of sin." (Rom. 7:25—Moffatt) All of us know that the mind most certainly controls our actions in the flesh; therefore, Paul must have meant that consciously he served the law of God, but with some of the unconscious, he served the law of sin. "Miserable wretch that I am!" he exclaimed. Then asked, "Who will rescue me?" His added answer was, "God will! Thanks be to Him through Jesus Christ our Lord." (Rom. 7:24-25—Moffatt) In other words, *we can subdue and convert the unconscious.*

Further evidence of the existence of our two minds is attested by the Psalmist in Psalms 16:7—"I thank the Eternal for His counsel, for *teaching me during the very night.*" (Moffatt) We think much of this teaching occurred while David was actually asleep. Such often happens with us. Have you ever gone to bed with some unsolved mathematical problem, or a similar one upon your mind, to awaken the next morning with the answer? This is due to your unconscious mind having worked it out for you while your conscious mind slept. The surgeon and his colleagues occasionally witness expressions from the unconscious minds of their patients. Groanings and some mumbled verbalizations will sometimes emerge from the patient on the operating table which he never recalls and of course was wholly unaware of. Moreover, it occasionally happens that a very religious person will mumble something that would embarrass him in the waking state, whereas the most wicked might offer a prayer. This is due to the inhibition of cerebral censorship (induced by the anesthesia, the conscious being asleep) which permits an occasional suppressed thought to emerge. Incidentally, this also points up the fact that down deep there is some suppressed good in the worst of us, and a little evil in the best of us.

Another modern demonstration of the two minds is evidenced in what is called "sleep teaching." The armed forces used it to some success during World War II in teaching some of our intelligence agents the Japanese language. It appeared to work in some cases and fail in others. The writer has likewise used it in helping distrought mothers deal with nocturnal enuresis (bedwetting) by children. During the first hour of sleep there is a period when a child can hear what is being whispered into the ear, and yet remain asleep. During this time, some suggestions and information are repeatedly given to the child by the mother which for example, may later cause him to awaken and avoid the bedwetting. (Needless to say, such therapy will not be the answer if there are organic or functional disorders. These must first be ruled out before a training process can begin.) We give these illustrations of the workings of the mind, to give meaning to what David asserted with reference to "God teaching him during the very night." We believe that David had both his conscious and unconscious mind literally invaded and filled, with the good things of God;

and therefore, whether asleep or awake—God taught
him! "In His law did he meditate both *day and night.*"

— CLEANSING OR CONVERTING THE UNCONSCIOUS —

If the aforementioned illustrations give additional
insight, the need is also apparent for an even better understanding of the unconscious in relation to the cleansing and conversion processes. For this additional insight,
it is necessary that we touch upon the mechanism of:

— REPRESSION —

Repression is simply the pushing into unawareness
those thoughts and impulses that are undesireable and
unwanted. We simply say—"Get back down into unawareness—I don't want to think about you, nor deal
with you at this time." Doing this comes about as naturally as a common reflex action. Of course, some repression is necessary for normal living, but the pay-off
comes when we maintain a pattern, of it, rather than
cleansing or converting the repressed unconscious material. When we simply fill up down below—something
has to give, and it usually results in some form of the
neuroses. The force responsible for maintaining repression is known as anxiety. The formula for all of the
aforementioned being: conflict—anxiety—repression—then
bodily symptoms. We mention these to permit the reader
to clearly see them in the spiritual counterpart to follow.
Before, however, we examine the spiritual aspect, we
shall risk bordom with another illustration.

Some years ago the author was lecturing along these
lines after which a pediatrician approached him with

the following problem. He had a child patient, perhaps eight or ten years of age, who was having great difficulty in attending school. Practically every morning just as soon as she arrived at school, she would begin to hysterically cry and shake with uncontrollable sobs. All the solace and efforts by both teachers and parents were inadequate in making it possible for the child to remain at school. When asked why she was crying and did not want to remain at school; her reply was always the same: "I don't know." And the fact was, she didn't know. After obtaining the clinical picture, we approached the solution by a consideration of "the antecedent theory of conflict"—that is, a search for some earlier psychological trauma in the child's life which she could be unconsciously equating with her school attendance. Here we found the answer. Suffice it to say, that we had learned from the parents that when she was about four or five years of age, they had left her with other children but under the care of a resort manager. When she discovered her parents were missing (even though they were only gone an hour or so) she became very frightened and practically remained in a hysterical condition until their return. Further investigation revealed that the child and siblings had often been left with the maid or butler during the absence of the parents. Some of these events had likewise been quite disturbing. All of them however, had been repressed, but now the child was unconsciously equating her leaving her parents and going to school with *their* leaving and going away; and thus she was unconsciously reliving all of these past undesirable experiences. When these were explained to her, together with some other important therapy, she soon adjusted to school and her trouble ceased. It points up the importance of dealing with what exists in the unconscious, and the need for cleansing. Now, let's examine the spiritual counterpart.

CONVERTING BOTH MINDS

In the above heading, we include the need for converting both our *actions and reactions*. Many of us are able to change some of our actions by ceasing the commission of overt sins such as lying, stealing, fornication, etc. but we often fail to come to grips with the undergirding of these and similar actions. It is what we are able to do with "what is below" that will determine how we react; and until this is done, we are at the mercy of the other fellow. Until we convert our reactions we can't live by our own decisions and choices, but only by the stimuli presented by external forces.

EXAMPLES OF VARIOUS REACTIONS:

Compare the reactions of Cain with those of Joseph, the son of Jacob. Killing his brother did not necessarily make Cain a bad man, indeed he was already bad at heart, and the slaying of his brother was the confirmation. When God required both Cain and Abel to present certain prescribed sacrifices, He simply evoked what was already in the hearts of both men. The soil of their hearts had long been cultivated before the slaying occurred. In contrast with Cain, let us note the reactions of Joseph.

It will be remembered that Joseph was sold into slavery by his own blood brothers. When these same brothers later visited Egypt to buy corn and were brought into his presence, he could have reacted by "getting even." He could have smiled, folded his arms and said, "Now get down on your bellies (like the snakes you are) and crawl up to me and beg." But he didn't and the reason was because this noble character had long been converted from such reactions. His reaction was tears— he wept! His weeping over the sins of others gave meaning to what Jesus later stated in the words "Blessed are they who mourn, for they shall be comforted." Joseph found that comfort.

In contrast to the reactions of Joseph, we note those of the elder son as related in the parable of the prodigal son found in Luke, chapter 15. An examination of this elder brother shows that he accurately personified mere "intellectual" and arrested conversion. He, had been delivered from the overt sins of prodigality but was uncleansed at the bottom. Needless to say, a man who can't rejoice and praise God at the redemption of a brother is obviously nothing more than a spiritual pigmy. Not only did he fail to rejoice, but he chose to refer to his brother as "this, *thy son*— (and-drag-it-by-slowly) who devoured thy living with harlots"; rather than "this, *my brother*" who was missed, needed and wanted. There is a difference in saying someone is *"your* son" and in saying he is *"my* brother."

Our reactions to how others affect us is comparable to the use of a hypodermic needle. We can let it either infect or inoculate us. We have often thought of how Simon and Cyrenian could have reacted after having been made to bear the cross. His skin was sufficiently dark, he was from another country and could have felt both persecuted and humiliated, and thus refused to have had anything to do with Christianity. Apparently he must have possessed balance and the ability to carefully weigh matters. The evidence shows that the cross apparently inoculated rather than infecting him, because his two sons, Rufus and Alexander, are prominently and favorably mentioned in Mark 15:21. We, too, can do one of two things with crosses—we can turn them into victory as did Simon, or reject them as burdens to be avoided by us, but borne by others.

If these few glaring reactions have emphasized the need for knowing better how to handle such rather simple and everyday stimuli of life, no doubt the reader has already anticipated our desire as well as the need for going yet deeper into the more complex problems. In doing this let us consider:

THE THREAD OF LIFE

Life is often referred to as a thread extending from birth to death. Let us try to visualize a thread or string with several scattered knots tightly tied in it. (See illustration)

A	x—x—x	B	o—o—o	C	z—z—z
Helplessness		Fears		Insecurity	

We shall refer to these knots as psychological traumas (trauma means wound) that are created by certain events in life. Events, shall we say, that literally tie us in knots. Early in life, maybe before birth, they began to appear. It is well known that the unborn are able to hear loud external noises, thus it is even possible that certain knots can begin during this period. While it is thought that we are born with only two fears—(loud noises and falling) —we can actually acquire about five thousand of them in an average lifetime. It will be readily seen then that more and more opportunities are always present for our acquiring other fears, frustrations and various knot tying experiences.

In order to better appreciate the knot tying processes it is well to consider some of the early and primary causes thereof. Some of these anxieties (unknown fears) along with the known fears and threats are: Feelings of helplessness, separation or the threat of it, privation and loss, fear of adult or significant disapproval, accidents and near accidents, extreme hunger, severe illness, various feelings of insecurity and a host of similar things are all capable of creating unforgetable knots in the string. (The reader may here recall the case of Phoebe, the little school girl previously mentioned.) All of these make lasting impressions upon the unconscious, but which the conscious may "forget" or repress over the years.

THE DISTURBANCE AND REACTIVATION OF THE KNOT CATEGORIES

One of the first things the mind does with knowledge is to classify it. This is a part of the memory process. By taking another look at the illustration of the string, it will be noted that we have accordingly classified the various knots into separate sections or categories. We have designated category A as knots having to do with feelings of helplessness, B as fears and C as insecurity. Now visualize the string being plucked at category B (fear). As a result of this stimulus (the plucking) all of the knots in that particular section would vibrate. In effect, all of them are stirred up and reactivated. This illustrates the fact that when certain traumatic knots are reactivated in a neurosis, we must unconsciously deal with all or at least some of them once again. Not being aware of this, most of us think of the last event as being the only thing bothering us and with which we must cope. On the other hand, it explains why apparently one single precipitating event can cause us to become completely upset, or precipitate an anxiety neurosis with full blown anxiety attack and panic. It is in such cases that it becomes necessary for the doctor to explain to the patient the relation between the precipitating cause and the many underlying causes. In other words, the focused and precipitating event "ran the cup over," but other similar things filled it up. The patient must see that he is unconsciously re-experiencing some of his past—that not one, but several blows are coming at the same time. When this is understood, it is often possible for the patient to calm down and understand that what is now affecting him is not actually a tornado, but perhaps several small winds simultaneously.

PHYSICAL REACTIONS

Accompanying many fear incidents, there occurs such physical sensations as feelings of the hair standing up—tightening of the skeletal muscles—goose pimples—et cetera. Whatever the first physical reaction (to fear incidents) the same will always be repeated unless of course we later condition ourselves to alter the response. For example, the writer can usually feel some skeletal muscles tighten when he is driving on icy roads. He was in an accident which was largely due to an unseen icy spot. He is yet subject to this particular conditioned response. These, and countless similar fears, all cause the physical fear category of the string of life to be affected. The effects will be in relation to our emotional vulnerability and the significance attached to the variety of the experiences. The manner and extent of our response is referred to as our T.R.C. (Total Response to Crisis). This is comparable to the manner in which fire fighting equipment responds to various types of alarms—i.e., the greater the fire, the more alarms are sounded. If however, the size of the fire is misjudged with more alarms continuing to sound, all the equipment will respond whether needed or not.

Correspondingly, if we misjudge our "fire" or emergency, our greater alarms will sound and we too, will respond out of proportion to the actual conditions. Therefore, our T.R.C. becomes a fairly accurate gauge of our vulnerability, resources, knowledge, experiences and emotional equipment, and of the manner in which we will handle the alarms of life. If our T.R.C. is out of proportion to life's stimuli, it is an indication that we are living in too much of a state of apprehension or alarm. Every moment will be one of "fight or flight." It will be noted in the spiritual counterpart both *why* and *how* some folk have developed too much of a T.R.C.— they are in a constant state of apprehension, alarm or battle. Practically everything is interpreted by them as some sort of threat. Some are conscious ones and others are wholly unrecognized.

HOW DO THE KNOTS AND THEIR REACTIVATION AFFECT US RELIGIOUSLY?

Whatever deeply affects us, also affects us spiritually in some way. There is positively no such thing as a "spiritual" and a "secular life." Life is just life, and there can be no compartmentalization or division of it. *What* we *believe* actually becomes "by-lief" or what we live by. The soma and psyche (body and mind) are so interrelated that in many illnesses man can be no longer considered properly diagnosed without consideration being given to possible psychosomatics. The scripture "As a man thinketh, so is he"—finds partial meaning here. The first lie detector (Numbers 5th chapter) proved the effect of the mind upon the body. The modern polygraph operates upon that principle. The principle being that lying is an attempt at reversing life's normal processes. If life cannot be divided, compartmentalized or reversed, it will be readily seen that what we may refer to as everyday normal fears, frustrations, anxieties, feelings of both security and insecurity, along with our emotional development and maturity, are most certainly going to affect us spiritually.

Let us first note the relationship of some of the aforementioned to:

— SPIRITUAL SECURITY —

In early life, security is associated with several things. Breast feeding is an example whereby food, warmth, rest and peace are realized. We never outgrow these emotional needs anymore than we do the need for food. In fact, the very psychology of sedation is to temporarily regress the patient toward this infantile state. Further evidence of this regression is seen in the bodily positions assumed in sleep wherein we coil or fold up as we did prior to birth. (In the womb our every need was satisfactorily met.)

From birth, all down through the years, measures

of security are likewise associated with or attached to certain things, places and persons. And threat to them, or deprivation thereof is likely to be interpreted as being disastrous to us. We won't surrender them without protest or maybe a fight. They constitute part of our roots which hold and anchor us. Some of these are recognized and some are unrecognized.

Perhaps the following illustration will help us appreciate the resistance to the pulling up of our roots of security, and, at the same time add a little insight relative to some of the problems of youth.

One of the many problems in clinical vogue today has to do with some of our young folk being in conflict with both parents and school. Some with whom we have talked are hostile, cynical, uncooperative and unappreciative with both the parents and the school. Fine Christian families are by no means excepted. Some young folk feel that their parents do not understand nor trust them, while of course they never dream that a part of this is a projection of some of their own self confusion and fear which they may be labeling as a shortage of trust or confidence. Often their lack of self confidence toward life situations, makes them feel that others (parents) also view them with a lack of confidence. "Don't you trust me?" is not uncommon.

In this early struggle toward emancipation (growing up) and flexing, there is the pressing desire for self assertiveness and reality testing. Sometimes, it appears that complete freedom without responsibility might sum up the desire. To attain these, however, other things must be threatened or even given up. To threaten our roots and anchors of home creates fear and apprehension (anxiety) which in turn greatly potentiates the frustration, conflict and fears, thus forcing the youngster to regressively cling to the from which he actually desires to be severed. Hence it creates a so-called vicious cycle which would appear in diagram as follows:

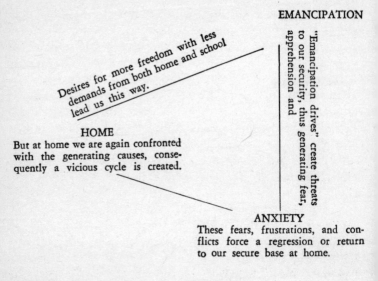

EMANCIPATION

Desires for more freedom with less demands from both home and school lead us this way.

"Emancipation drives" create threats to our security, thus generating fear, apprehension and

HOME
But at home we are again confronted with the generating causes, consequently a vicious cycle is created.

ANXIETY
These fears, frustrations, and conflicts force a regression or return to our secure base at home.

Actually, the conflict is due to two opposing desires. The desire to gain freedom and the desire to hold on to home for the security roots and anchors so badly needed. It will be seen then, that the very youngster who consciously thinks he wants to uproot and unanchor himself, will unconsciously fight to hold on to them. He becomes rebellious, cynical, nervous and even depressed. The "joke" is, they often blame parents and/or school for their problem. School is a factor because it is interpreted as an extension of the home, i.e., authority, demands, (do's and don'ts) with threats of poor grades, failures, etc.

172

— THE SPIRITUAL COUNTERPART —

Now, just as these youngsters find themselves consciously desiring one thing, yet unconsciously something else; we too are caught with two similar, though very important spiritual strivings. The desire for growth, progress and expression, yet within *anchors and frameworks of thinking, beliefs and practices which to us constitute approbation of God and spiritual security.* For some, it is indeed religiously frustrating to attempt to become *"geared to the times, while anchored to the Rock."* To these, change itself, nearly always creates fear. Fear of "popularity, modernism, drifting"—and ultimate damnation. Consequently, they follow a very, very conservative procedure in almost all things.

— FORMATION OF SPIRITUAL ANCHORS —

The formation and perpetuity of our spiritual roots and anchors are about as closely related to *where* and by *whom* we were taught, as they are to the *"what."* To some of us, the "whom" is all important, else there would be few so-called traditional religious concepts, and yet fewer sensitivities when they are challenged or even mentioned. Hence, if a certain preacher states something as a fact,—it is "law and gospel" to many. The *whom* is the authority. Likewise, the locale or place where our roots were established is an important factor. The home congregation, where early impressions were made and precious memories created, are also roots that have to be challenged or maybe pulled up when a change of some long held and cherished religious belief is to be made. All of the aforementioned serve to potentiate what was learned and emotionally accepted. Security, locale and memories, together with nostalgic warmth are all associated with our anchors, and even self autonomy and the self image. Hence, to change a religious view cannot only mean the pulling up of some roots of security, it can likewise involve some surrender of authority, power, and ego image. Needless to say, only the relatively mature can meet such challenges and make the necessary changes with balance and poise.

To the rigid, inflexible and unbending person (evidences of immaturity within themselves) such a procedure would spell catastrophe. This type individual would regard a change in method or protocol as "surrendering everything," "*letting down the bars,*" the "*tendency to drift*"—"*drifting,*" "*modernism,*" *etc*. To him, progress is necessarily limited to only what he can emotionally accept. Anything beyond that is "drifting and dreaming." That is why we mentioned the fear of the space age in our first chapter. With reference to this very thing, this decade will to some be the "soaring 60's" and to others the "souring of the milky way!" Depending upon what we are emotionally ready to accept. But here the question could arise "what does all of this have to do with conversion, especially of the unconscious?" This—It is hoped that if we can gain more self insight, we may be better able to approach and evaluate such matters as religious unity, peace and joy in the Holy Spirit. No one can intelligently approach such subjects as fellowship, unity, world wide missions and benevolent work unless he at least has an inkling with reference to *latent* hindrances. These hindrances can partially be attributed to some of us consciously wanting more light, yet unconsciously rejecting it.

If we can learn what we have heretofore stated,

namely, that conversion is a continual process and consequently *convert some emotions as well as ideas,* we can proceed by carefully weighed decisions rather than by reactions. We will make ourselves and the world see New Testament Christianity as the religion worth having. Neither Heaven nor the world would any longer look upon us as perhaps a well-meaning but comparatively ignorant people trying to enlighten the entire world, while we have largely failed to even examine the bottom of our own souls.

Moreover, our continually evaluating and dealing with our emotional blind spots will create much better relations. For example, a preacher who in his early years saw his father as a domineering boss or maybe a "tyrant" will be keenly aware of the possibility, if not even the likelihood of his projection of his father with continued reaction to him in working with the elders of the congregation.

Likewise, an elder who most of his life has possessed inferior feelings and unrecognized emotional needs, might become more able to see the possibilities of his resenting other men being appointed to that office, especially of he feels these newer men are superior to him. Indeed, there are few of them who yield to saying "Brother, you are a better man than I, you will do a superior job. Therefore, I'll step out graciously, but continue my interest and efforts."

The writer recalls an incident where a former elder's daughter stated: "They are asking my father to resign the greatest *honor* in the world." Actually the man had not met with the flock in a year. He knew he wasn't an elder anymore than he was Jesus Christ, but he couldn't emotionally surrender what to him was honor, authority, prestige and power. This would shatter his self-image.

Moreover, if more self insight were possessed there would be less arguing and fighting among so many good people who honestly think they want to advance the kingdom of God. Much of the opposition to any form of progress comes from some of us who *absolutely do not know* why we oppose something. We just think we do. Much of it is to gain attention and perhaps prominence. A man who can "stop the tide and save the church" is certain to be a hero and champion to some. If, by chance, some "fellow parrots" can join the fight with him, they too, enlarge the self image by identification and incorporation and perhaps see themselves as great men of destiny. Some of this has long been recognized and evidenced by those who, when beginning some special effort, will "clear it" or "get advice" from people whom they publically approve with private contempt. By "consulting" the probable opposition it is hoped that there will be none. Some of these people don't love one another, as they claim they do. What they would call love is nothing more than domesticated resentments. Real love will cause us to accept the challenge and responsibilities of trying to understand and make something worthwhile out of each other. Real love cannot operate until domesticated hate and resentments, along with love choices and hate substitutes are brought into awarenes sand effectively dealt with.

There must be continual conversion as long as there is continual perversion, and most of the perversion will come from well meaning people who honestly feel they "have arrived."

Chapter 11

COUNSELLING THE EMOTIONALLY DISTURBED

— INTRODUCTION —

This chapter is intended as a special supplement for ministers and those of his staff who may be lending a sympathetic hand in this direction. The writer is convinced from his own experiences and clinical records, that a good minister with keen insight and sympathetic understanding can give some special help in many cases which an everyday psychiatrist could never proffer. We believe this for the simple reason that anyone who effectively deals with interpersonal relationship must eventually come to grips with values—indeed, a standard of spiritual value. Too often the everyday psychiatrist is lacking in these and as a result, he can do as much harm as good. To go further, you may place us on record as believing that every doctor engaged in the practice of psychiatry should hold a sound faith in the living God and in His word, the Bible. (Idealistic we admit). Along with this, we also assert that thert is not one "sound, tried and true" psychiatric concept with which there is Biblical conflict. The belief that there must necessarily be conflict between the Christian religion and true dynamic psychiatry is false. There may be conflict with some religions and even a distorted Christianity, but

177

never with the genuine. They complement one another and both definitely have their place.

— CONTROL BY DIRECTION —

Every normal person must live by some sort of control if healthy living is to be enjoyed, and the best control yet discovered is that of Christ which in turn is the only known control with absolute freedom. Freedom in every sense of its meaning. Paul therefore speaks of it: "The interests of the Spirit mean life and peace (Rom. 7:6—Moffatt) He also adds "The harvest (the reaping) of the Spirit in love, joy, peace, good temper, kindliness, generosity, fidelity, gentleness, self control" (Gal. 5:22—Moffatt) Now place these before any truly qualified psychiatrist and ask him to write a book on the Meaning of Emotional Health while excluding these as a part of his spectrum. He couldn't get any farther than the first word—Love! In fact one says that we must "Love or Perish" and proves it with a vengeance.*

What we are stating is by no means intended to downgrade psychiatry, but to upgrade its plentiful counterparts in the word of God, and recognize the skilful minister who knows how to handle them. As we have stated elsewhere, Christian psychotherapy is not a substitute for psychiatry, but usually a part of it. That part in many cases may be a much needed and new purpose for life. And this comes only by one's alignment with The Life.

A WORD OF CAUTION

Our intended good in this chapter could easily re-

———
* "Love or Perish"—By Smiley Blanton, M.D.

sult in harm if the average reader, after digesting this, should feel that it qualifies him for anything more than a listening and guidepost for those who come to him for help. Interpersonal relationships are both delicate and potent, and superficiality of knowledge is dangerous in this realm. In dealing with some of the various aspects of the neuroses, let us be careful to remain within safe boundaries lest we create more anxiety and other problems than we can handle. This is especially true with the schizophrenic type patient and some others who by all means should be *altogethe*r left in better skilled and trained hands. In these cases, a sympathetic listening ear with genuine interest and understanding fills a very great need.

Another caution must be observed with reference to depressed people and those with rather strong feeling of guilt. Many times these patients seek help from the minister in attempts to alleviate their guilt. Quite frequently, they begin to doubt the validity of their baptism (we speak particularly of those who are members of the Church of Christ) and as a result they finally get around to asking their preacher how he views "re-baptism." Preacher, don't fall into a "trap" at this point. Due to our emphasis of Acts 2:38 (efficacy of baptism) the patient may feel that "re-baptism" is the answer, but it seldom is. Consequently, if the patient is again immersed and the guilt feelings continue, (which they likely will) more guilt will be created and the patient will feel even worse. This is because he feels that as he tries to get closer to God—the Father backs away. We refer to this as "neurotic" guilt. Consequently he interprets all of this as additional evidence of his guilt and the load increases. When this happens, the patient's faith is weakened because already he feels his prayers are going unheard and now even "baptism failed"!

Needless to say, unless the minister has some pretty good insight into guilt formations and patterns, he had best simply ask the disturbed person to accept his word that Christians can most certainly experience emotional disturbances with guilt feelings, that such are not necessarily the result of sin, and by all means not a retribution from God. With this he can then refer the party to the proper sources of help. If, however, the counsellor has a few illustrations for insight which he can share with the patient, instead of soberly concluding, "Yes, we're all sinners"—(which does no good at all) it is likely the patient will leave his office with a lighter load and better anticipation toward the referral. Nor must we overlook the "unconscious and conscious image" in which the minister is held even by members of the Church of Christ. Most likely the patient projects some of both his father and The Father in such interviews (images of security, power and magic). Nor should the strong possibility for the need of unconscious atonement on the part of the patient be overlooked. To jerk this emotional need away can result in its replacement by something worse. In other words some people simply "cannot recover" until they have unconsciously "paid the fare." This is one of the psychotherapeutic values of E.S.T. (electro-shock treatment). The patient often equates it with death and atonement and therefore feels both capable and willing, as well as worthy, of starting life anew.

ANXIETY

I.

    (a) *EFFORTS TO AVOID ANXIETY*—Man by his

very nature seeks to avoid that which is unacceptable or threatening to him. This will be more fully discussed under the mechanism of repression but for the time being it will suffice to say that our seeking to avoid anxiety is the beginning of our attempts to cover up our fears and intolerable thoughts that seek to come into conscious awareness.

(b) *A FORMULA* — Conflict-Anxiety-Repression = Symptoms

The above shows how the neuroses become the "harvest of conflict." When the ego fails to integrate our drives, needs, strivings, etc.; in a manner compatible with the superego, the conflict ensues.

II.

(a) *NATURE OF ANXIETY — THE UNIVERSALITY OF IT* — A certain amount of it is necessary for normal living—hence it is universal. Inasmuch as all of us at some time or other possess thoughts, impulses, and ideas which are unacceptable, the forces of anxiety arise and brings about repression in our attempts to forget or push the unwanted ones out of conscious awareness. Usually this amounts to our tucking them away in the unconscious.

(b) *ANXIETY IS OF VALUE.* It causes us to seek help. It ceases to be an asset when it causes us to develop a too potent T.R.C. (Total Response to Crisis) and interferes with normal living.

181

(c) *T.R.C.* — our total response to crisis refers to our physical, psychological, emotional, spiritual and mental response to certain threats or danger. It too, is vitally necessary and only becomes a liability when the response is out of proportion to the stimulus. For example, we are driving along and suddenly a man runs from the sidewalk and jumps a fence over into a neighbor's yard. When asked why he did it, he replies "I was once brushed by a car and now when a horn blows I intend to get out of the way." Obviously, his T.R.C. to fears of automobiles and traffic is too great.

(d) *RELIGIOUS CONCEPTS AND ANXIETY*. Anxiety can also be caused by faulty or ill conceived religious concepts. Preaching and teaching can create much anxiety and neurotic guilt if God and His will are presented in such a way as to cause a wrong type of fear instead of genuine awe. Such can also produce needless hypersensitivity toward His teachings in the Bible. (What we have heretofore referred to as absolutism and one-hundred-per-cent scripturalness.) As stated elsewhere, every normal being must live with a normal amount of control to enjoy normal emotional health. In view of this it will be noted that *any system of instruction which would only tend to convert the top of the mind and miss the bottom of the soul would result in religious conflict, frustration and neurosis.* Moreover, it usually results in spiritual abortion as well. This is dealt with in the chapter on Conversion.

III. MANIFESTATIONS OF ANXIETY

   (a) Nervousness, tension,

   (b) Certain motor disturbances, speech difficulties, sleep disturbance, insomnia, disturbing dreams, interference with mental functions, impaired attention and concentration, restlessness, tremors, angry outbursts and terrific T.R.C. reactions.

   (c) Indirect manifestations—psychologic conversion resulting in phobias, depression, dissociative reactions, hypochondriasis, obsessions, compulsions, and extreme fatigue.

IV. SOME MENTAL MECHANISMS

Denial, displacement, dissociation, fantasy, identification, projection inversion, retionalization, reaction formation, regression, repression symbolization, fainting, replacement etc., all which may be labeled as Intrapsychic Defense Mechanisms. These are a few attempted defenses by which the patient seeks to reach solutions and/or compromise. The last mentioned is usually the result.

V. SOME SOURCES OF ANXIETY

These begin in infancy and early childhood and perhaps in some cases before birth. (Loud noises may be heard before birth.)

   (a) Separation, frustration, helplessness, privation, communicable anxiety derived from identification with parents, fear of disapproval from parents and other significant adults (teachers, coaches etc.), physical pain, accidents, family discord, illness, extreme thirst and hunger.

VI. ANXIETY REACTIONS— (Psychological)

Having already noted some direct manifestations, we present Case No. 44-W as an example. This person sought help because of an anxiety attack while driving. He related how he began to tremble with fright accompanied by hyperventilation (breathing fast and deeply). The patient parked his car then lost consciousness. Upon regaining consciousness he was pleasantly surprised to be alive even though he was yet greatly alarmed.

Much of his apprehension of another attack was allayed by an explanation of hyperventilation. (Wherein we retain too much oxygen at the expense of carbon dioxide. Breathing into a paper bag will alleviate the problem). To this one we could add several other reactions including: anxiety panic, anxiety hysteria, anxiety tension, etc.

PHOBIAS

Definition: "A phobia is a fear, usually very much out of proportion to the stimulus, which is attached to an external object symbolizing internal fear of something else. The gulf of difference between recognized fear and a phobia is evidenced by the unreasonableness of the last mentioned. For example, everyone knows that thunder harms no one, yet brontophobia (fear of thunder) is not uncommon.

Through the phobia the patient is able to conceal from conscious awareness the real internal fear, threat, or danger. The inner fear is unconsciously transferred to the phobic object by the mechanism of displacement. Needless to say, the patient has a very strong conscious desire to rid himself of the phobia, but an even stronger *unconscious* desire to retain it. If he could have dealt with the internal fear to begin with, the external symbolization would never have been developed. Hence, the doctor who has to delicately and sympathetically handle such cases faces a tremendous task, because the patient honestly feels he wants help, but he may be fighting with all of his power to retain his phobia. His holding on to it is due to what is known as the endogain (primary benefits) which the phobia represents to him. It can be readily seen that should the therapist at once recognize with absolute certainty what the phobia represented to the patient, it could result in near disaster if he prematurely revealed it before the patient could emotionally accept the answer. This will also point up the possible danger of hypnotism in untrained hands. An untrained person might well think he is helping by removing the symptom when actually he would likely be doing great harm. Symptom removal in some cases can actually precipitate a frank psychosis. The writer bases this upon his own clinical observations, the reports of competent certified psychiatrists, and his own training in this particular branch of medical psychology. Moreover, he has been led to the conclusion that perhaps in most all cases where interpersonal relationships are of much clinical significance, the use of this "tool" should be left for the experienced psychiatrist. Phobias, like all other expressions of the neuroses are for skilled hands and once again we point out the role of the minister as a pointing hand in this direction.

— DEPRESSION —

Our reference here is to emotional depression which is expressed by dejection, sadness, lowering of the mood or spirits, melancholy etc. There are various types of depression but the outward expressions are about the same for all. The depressed person is not difficult to identify.

— CAUSES —

We feel that failure of adaptation and the use of depression as a very strong defense mechanism against anxiety are perhaps the main causal factors. Failure of adaptation occurs when one is unable to make his past experiences and life's accumulations fit into his environment. If he is unable to accomplish this, he will in turn regress to earlier acceptable patterns. Because his whole personality (i.e. the whole of him) does not participate in the regression (perhaps the most part is striving to progress and adapt) conflict develops, feelings of futility emerge and he feels inadequate toward life's situations. Obviously, such a person shows an abundance of vulnerable spots that have been accumulated over the years which seem to predispose or "cast" him as a type of depressed or dejected personality. Had he been able to have developed satisfactorily mature relationships during this time, his psychological foundations and undergirdings would not have permitted the erection of such a depressed superstructure.

It is in view of these type undergirdings, that we feel some women are somewhat predisposed to a variety of symtomatology while experiencing some endocrine (hormonal) imbalance during the menopause.

In other words, the woman who has fairly solid psychological undergirdings is likely to make this transition with a minimum of discomfort or maybe none at all.

— DEPRESSION: AS A STRONG DEFENSE MECHANISM AGAINST ANXIETY —

This type of depression is about as deep and potent as any to be noted. When rather strong anxiety is to be coped with, a correspondingly strong defense must be erected for protection against it. Consequently, one may fairly accurately judge the potency or "charge" of the unconscious threat or fear by the depth of the depression. It is usually in exact proportion to the dread, fear, threat or apprehensiveness in the anxiety core. This being true it is at once seen how the person would naturally "defend his defense" because his depression represents a crutch without which the patient feels he would collapse. Consciously he wants to alleviate the depression, but unconsciously he wants to retain it. This is why it is so silly or maybe downright cruel for well meaning people to exhort some depressed soul to "Snap out of it"! Moreover, the "peelings of positive thinking" will not produce the magical snap. Proper concepts can point us in the right direction and maybe help us in *certain* areas, but it takes more than books to get results—else patients would be handed them with the suggestion: "Heal thyself." And let us hasten to add that even insight therapy alone is not usually sufficient. The insight *must* become a core together with *action* by the patient in order to bring about satisfactory adaptation and relationships.

Psychiatry in general regards the type of depression under discussion as "a last stand defense against anxiety."

187

For this reason, it is important that the minister and family be aware of the most *serious level* of the depression. This is *NOT WHEN THE PATIENT HITS THE BOTTOM, but afterwards when improvement seems so apparent.* What the untrained and inexperienced do not understand is that suicide is most likely when the patient seems to be starting upward. When at the very bottom of the depression the patient literally just does not have the "get up and do it" will or strength to carry out the act. This is another reason why cooperation with the attending physician is so very important. He is ever cognizant of these possibilities but does not have time to explain all of his decisions and actions to everyone.

We therefore mention a few of them so that when the minister is perhaps approached by the family together with the patient, he will not react to a false sense of security evidenced by any or all parties and maybe falter in encouraging a "stick to your doctor" program. A minister would indeed feel badly if he should agree that the patient appeared so much improved that maybe further hospitalization and treatment seemed unnecessary, only to find himslf being asked in a few days to conduct a funeral. Many are the times when the patient will so dread further treatment (especially E.S.T.) that the family along with the patient will turn to the minister for support and counsel. The patient will often ask, "Do *you* really think I need further treatment?" The safest reply is, "Your doctor knows better than anyone else and I would abide by his decisions. If however you insist, I will talk with him about it and give you our opinions later." Any good doctor will appreciate both the minister's position and interest, and will gladly accept your help as a colleague. First, because of ordinary professional courtesy, and secondly because the so-called "men in white and the men in black" are finding out that they are on the same team. This is particularly true where psychiatrists know that certain ministers possess good insight and perhaps some training. We must admit however that many doctors would frankly piefer their patients not consult some ministers. On the whole however the relationship is very good.

— DEPRESSION VIA SUCCESS —

Here is one of the most unusual aspects of depression and occasionally quite deceiving for almost everyone. It results when success is very much apparent, yet unconsciously represents a most important loss to the person.

Success is sometimes equated with vanquishing the foe (as in athletics) annihilating, outdoing, destroying something or someone. Earlier prototypes may have included loved ones or greatly respected persons, who in many or maybe all cases may have been someone upon whom the subject was very dependent. Consequently, when the triumph of success occurs these antecedents are all reactivated and the patient feels he has vanquished something or someone very dear or necessary to him. He is therefore depressed and likely feels guilty. The writer recalls having seen this in a fine general practitioner, who decided to take up surgery altogether. In the same small town was a colleague (G.P.) who was highly respected, admired and regarded somewhat as a brother by the depressed physician. In dinner conversation with the surgeon (he ate very little) our solicited opinion suggested that his specializing in surgery was being unconsciously interpreted as outdoing, vanquishing, or even annihilating his close friend and colleague. This also meant (as he interpreted it) a loss of friendship (a very severe loss) with accompanying guilt for causing it. I recall that on the following day when we made a call together, the man actually shed tears as we discussed it further. In our opinion, here was a case of "depression by success" in professional pageantry. Incidentally, it revealed a vulnerable spot which this fine doctor never dreamed of until he was "hit."

Similarly, a minister may be quite often confronted by brethren who appear to be "going places"—yet who frankly confess to him that they are tired, dejected and depressed. They are also likely to admit that their spiritual and even interpersonal relations are impaired. The very nature of our somewhat aggressive society contributes to this and it is seen quite frequently in salesmen. This is because this group often equates their making a sale with aggression. Psychiatry interprets some of the "dry spells" or periods of time when sales decline, as periods of recuperation from unconscious guilt by the salesman. In this way he atones for his aggression. It is our personal feeling that some insight along this line could help some Christian salespeople over their "hump" or "dry spells"!

Obviously, our touching upon the "depression from success" is to give the minister additional insight as to why some members may be knocking at his door when apparently everything is going fine. It may also enhance our understanding as to why this same person may not be as energetic in church work as before. The depression overlaps into all facets of his life. This type depression is a paradox and its consequences, as we see, can well present paradoxes which can make both ministers and elders "scratch their heads."

— OBSESSIONS AND COMPULSIONS —

DEFINITIONS—An obsession is an unwanted thought that seems to be ever present in conscious awareness. It, too, is another expression of the neuroses, potent with emotional significance, and may be considered as a defense mechanism against anxiety.

A compulsion is an unwanted urge to perform an act which is contrary to the individual's wishes. It too, is highly potent with emotional significance and is similarly a defense against anxiety—anxiety which is caused by an urge to perform or commit that which the compulsion represents and which is most intolerable to the patient.

— SOME MANIFESTATIONS —

We have personally witnessed no greater misery than patients with obsessive and/or compulsive thoughts in regard to harming loved ones. Anxiety panic, anxiety hysteria, or anxiety attack may be more alarming, but there is respite from these where there often appears to be none in the severe obsessions and compulsions.

The minister who is confronted with these will likely meet pople who are ashamed to reveal some of their thoughts. Moreover, they may often feel they are being "punished by God." Occasionally, we have actually been told by well meaning but pitifully uninformed people and their families, that the "victim appears to have a devil." Needless to say, the role of the counselor in such cases is clear cut! First, let it be *a kind but emphatic* statement that such is not the case. A long Biblical explanation is usually unnecessary.

Perhaps, the next step would be that of some explanation of defense mechanisms. Give the person a little sedatory information, with the assurance that his doctor will explain things more in detail. Above all, try and cause the person to understand that these feelings are neither punitive, nor from God, but that they represent unconscious material which a competent physician should discuss with them. Explain that a variety of things which happen to us in a lifetime affect us in various ways and that sometimes an accumulation of them will emerge into our conscious awareness just as twisted and nonsensical as some dreams. Be sympathetic, understanding, unalarmed, calm, poised and confident. This is contagious via identification of the patient with you as a symbol of security.

HELPFUL HINTS ON THE OBSESSIONS

1. The conflicts engendering these are largely due to early conditions and experiences in relationships with parents and other important adults. We feel that the first conflicts (relating to obsessions—not just first conflict) perhaps begin with the anal period where at least two types of handling are noted. In one the toilet functions have been greatly overemphasized in a positive sense, which often leads to pampering and the creation of a "pleasure activity" with the act. On the other hand a child may be subjected to a much too vigorous training with accompanying excessive discipline. This, of course, turns it into a battle ground where he must fight it out with "authority." We need not remind our readers how quickly some

children seize these functions as weapons to be used as symbols of their own authority or self-assertiveness. It is for this reason that most bed-wetting, for example, is not the fault of the child, but of the parents. They usually do not understand the child and do not seek the necessary help. Our advice to parents, especially to those who may be over concerned about proper handling, would be to simply avoid extremes. Most of us have common sense and that road is usually broad enough in any field for all of us who are not given to extreme wobbling.

2. The second battle is usually considered as beginning at puberty. At this stage rather strong impulses often have to be properly dealt with and here again there is some conflict with authority, superego, etc. This period will reactivate the former conflicts and pleasures, due to the same nerves being involved (actually they control) in the anal and other sensitive areas—the areas that were also stimulated in early childhood bath and hygiene procedures.

3. NEXT PHASE—Emerging out of the previous conflicts and other similar and potentiating experiences may later come a character of stubborness, orderliness, meticulousness and cleanliness. These serve to symbolically protect the patient from attack. In this way he is ever "on guard" and attempts to avoid being overwhelmed or even destroyed. He also hopes to avoid perfectionistic demands by others. The last mentioned, he interprets as domination which in turn causes fear and hatred. His stubborness will prevent a personal invasion of him, and this somewhat suggests the reasons for his

OBSTINACY—Here again one seeks to preserve intactness by refusing to yield anything. His miserliness and desires to accumulate and hold on to everything—like his stubborness; serve to keep things within himself. In our experiences we have seen these very symbols "transferred" or converted into physiological expressions in the forms of constricted oral and anal sphincters, along with spasticity in other areas. These psychosomatics are interpreted as an attempt on the part of some people to simply shut themselves off from certain threats or even the world.

REACTION FORMATIONS—Perhaps it is needless to say that usually the person so characterized has much hostility. Hardly ever does the average patient recognize this. He is unaware that his reaction formations of apparent meekness, along with ingratiation and submissiveness are all actually masking his hostility. The fear of harming or being harmed—or even killing or being killed, is almost always an unrecognized fear of the obsessive person. Thus, the aforementioned "shams" help to quiet and subdue these fears. The fears also potentiate his needs for

DEPENDENCY—The obsessive individual feels that he can only function if he is dependent upon someone else. He is "afraid of his own anger and powers of destruction," and the retaliation therefrom; and therefore, experiences much anxiety about being separated from a dependency source. Such separation means that he is "cut loose" and anything can happen to him or anyone else. He is like the individual (for our comparative purposes only) who expresses an abnormal fear in "not getting too close to a cliff because he fears he might lose control and jump against his wishes."

194

Another aspect of the dependency need is represented by the fantasies relative to those upon whom the patient is so dependent. These fantasies, like the resentment and hostility, are often equated with harming or killing. This is because the dependency is interpreted as subjection to domination or tyranny. The patient desires "to get rid of" or annihilate the "tyranny" but because of his being so dependent he must *repress* the undesirable unconscious impulses lest they come into conscious awareness. This in turn arouses the necessary amount of anxiety (the force responsible for maintaining repression) and once again the tormenting and vicious cycle is potentiated. It remains until proper and often extended therapy is utilized.

The preacher of course would never attempt to initiate therapy in such cases, but it is well to know that the patient will have an unrecognized barrier when he seeks your advice and help. That is, he would also like to be dependent upon you, as he would his physician, but feels that if he gets too close he might have to give up some of his defenses. By this, we mean that he defends his defense mechanisms. Hence, one should not feel that the person is uncooperative and wasting time if ambivalence and the heretofore mentioned obstinacy is observed.

Here again, we suggest the understanding that obsessions and compulsions are expression of the anxiety neuroses core, and are also reactions, conversions and mechanisms that have been desperately developed to allay or control the *concealed* fears or threats.

Chapter 12

— SOME GOALS AND PRINCIPLES OF GOOD PSYCHOTHERAPY —

1. *Improvement of adaptation*—As pointed out elsewhere, a neurosis often develops when the individual finds it impossible to adjust or adapt to his environment. We include the home, work, school, married life, economic conditions, racial problems, threat of war, etc., —everything the world presents. When this adaptation fails (failure of ego function) frustration and conflict occur because the total personality does not participate. Part of the person is trying to adapt, and part of him is "pulling back" and regressing to antecedent patterns, methods, or adjustments which the unparticipating (often arrested) part finds more acceptable. (Once again we see triumphant living and not just existing as a matter of total relationships and that improvement of these must often begin with the establishment of better communications and ordinary relationship with people.) Let it be remembered that there is no stopping place in psychotherapy—a patient either continues to improve and reach a satisfactory recovery or he regresses! Consequently, the improvement along the lines just mentioned are imperative. This often begins in a rather meager way. As an example, we have seen cases where those who had previously lost contact with reality began "the

road back" by simply glueing spools together. When they began to gain confidence in their ability to deal with "things," there was an accompanying confidence in their relationships or dealings with people. These were of course institutional cases which the average minister, or even doctor, would seldom encounter; but they point up the simple steps that are often prerequisites to greater strides. This principle would hold true in all of the neuroses, simply because the difference in the neurotic (any emotional illness) and the psychotic (where reality is lost) *is only in degree* and *not in kind*. Hence, it will be seen that many times the minister can especially provide the needed encouragement and "occupational therapy" (a job of some kind) which can be so very helpful to both the patient and others. Perhaps, we need not repeat that our happiness is derived from what we make happen to others, and not what happens to us. Consequently, what the counselled person can do for others will be of inestimatable value to him and especially his self image.

II. *Self Acceptance*—It is generally conceded that one can meet the ordinary winds of life with the few tornadoes, providing his self-image (how he views self) remains acceptable. For many, self acceptance is not easy. We are constantly being proded to improve, and to some of the hypersensitive, this is equated with their being defective—else why the need for improvement! This type person is always quite critical of self, rather unbending or inflexible and likely perfectionistic in self demands. They have fed themselves for so long on their own diet of self depreciation that they are full of "grasshopper complexes." The children of Israel, it will be recalled, looked upon themselves as grasshoppers in comparison to their enemies (Numbers 13) and their generation never fully recovered from the complex. About all of them died in the wilderness because they felt that even with God's help they could never conquer the enemy. Like some of us, they didn't wholly reject God.—They simply reduced Him.

An important ingredient of self acceptance is that of *some genuine self respect*. Many of us actually fail to see ourselves as others approvingly see us, hence there is quite an unnecessary discrepancy. David was a victim of this. Long after God had forgiven him, he refused to forgive himself. In Psalms 51:3 we read "Well do I know my offences; *my sin is never out of my mind.*" (Moffatt)

Let it be remembered that just as there are many who have far "worse *troubles*" than any of us, there are likewise people who are also *actually "worse"* than some of us. Let's ask ourselves this question, "Are we trying to be a part of the problem or a part of the answer?" Needless to say, anyone who "isn't on the wrong team is on the right one" so why not recognize our worth as others see us and "raise our heads!" After all, none of us appear exactly as we would like, else after "diddling" with or seeing dime store photography, we would not exclaim, "Well, *that* doesn't look like me, does it?" What we are actually saying is, "I don't want to recognize the fact that I look like that!" But, we plod on anyhow and blame the cheap photography. Well, humble soul— let's be as tolerant with our own "mental photographic equipment"!

Internal Improvement—Perhaps when some of the aforementioned are digested we may find ourslves more willing and better able to admit some of the inner conflicts, with better resolution and purpose. We recall an individual who had been rather harsh with herself because she thought her normal sexual interests were sinful. Her rearing with a lack of training in this respect had helped her form a rather harsh superego, and resultingly she had ignorantly placed herself on the animal level (as she referred to it) simply because she felt a wee bit sexually aggressive toward her husband. This woman was a member of a very strict "holiness" group, wore long sleeves, long hair and no makeup. She felt herself to depict holiness on the outside and vulgarity on the inner. Internal improvement and understanding along these lines naturally resulted in both a better self image and self acceptance.

In so many cases, we have found religious people (of many faiths) denying these normal sexual interests just as practically all of us deny our normal hostility. This, of course, points up the great need for proper Christian teaching and training on these very subjects. It can prevent a world of trouble.

— REASSURANCE —

One of the greatest worries expressed in most all forms of emotional illnesses is that of losing the mind. Regardless of the degree of the illness this fear lurks in the mind of most all patients. It is likely to be one of the first statements or questions offered by a patient. Here the minister can give great reassurance, especially when he has some insight into the individual's particular problem and can maybe explain a few primary, yet highly important facets of it. Naturally, an individual is going to be greatly agitated, worried and scared when a phobia, compulsion, or anxiety attack breaks through upon him. We need not comment upon "fear of the un-

199

known." Frankly, most any normal person experiencing any of these would likely wonder, "Am I losing my mind?" How would the reader feel if he should develop rather suddenly a strong phobia of traveling for no apparent reason whatsoever? Or, maybe an almost overwhelming fear of death? How would the average newlyweds feel should the husband develop a rather strong phobia of living with his wife for absolutely no apparent reason? Neither of them would likely entertain the possibility of the cause being his unconscious fear of vulnerability and hurt through such a close relationship. We have observed a case or two wherein a party had been previously "hurt" by a loved one or real close friend. Later on, the marriage relationship served to reactivate the earlier trauma. The closeness or intimacies of marriage in respect to the sharing of secrets, business, finances, and past experiences; bared certain vulnerable areas heretofore never seriously threatened. Baring these meant that the party could be "hurt" again, hence anxiety (unrecognized apprehension or fear) was created because of such very close relationships. In these, as in perhaps most all cases, some reassurance by the minister and prompt referral to the family physician can be as valuable as a beacon in the darkest night.

RE-EVALUATION OF PERSONAL GOALS

Sometimes we all find ourselves being more idealistic than realistic. Idealistic and fantasy concepts are the companions of youth as all parents well know. The solution later becomes more acceptable to all concerned by our being realistic about great ideals. It is certainly worthwhile to have high and noble ideals, but it is frankly pitiful when we become absolutely unbending, inflexible, and unyielding in our desire to excel. When anyone attempts to go beyond *honest integrity of effort,* he is there and then attempting what neither God nor sane people expect of him. He is already beginning "to think more highly *for* himself than he ought to think." The highway of life is literally littered with people who could never take a sane view of themselves, nor their aims and goals of life. Parents have contributed no little to it by their trying to fulfill their own ambitions and emotional needs through their children. In one city where the writer has lived he saw so many college freshmen in frustration and conflict that he instituted a file captioned "Freshmen Neuroses." We recall one rather pathetic girl who had to stay in the same dorm, occupy the same room, use the same desk and belong to the same sorority as Mom. When we were asked by the mother why her daughter seemed to be experiencing some trouble and desiring to quit college, our reply was: "When the old Mother hen stops hovering, pulls in her wing and stops clucking; the chick can pick it's own corn and gravel of life." And now Madam if you're ready to wean both yourself and your daughter, we think she will enjoy some reality testing for herself. Finally, you just try to be "the friend who stands by"! The girl felt she could never reach the goals her mother had set for her, thus her trouble began. Obviously, re-evaluation by both mother and daughter (especially mom) was vitally necessary.

Christian psychotherapy should point out that success by the evaluation of both Heaven and thinking Christian people *is not ascertained by the standards of men.* Jesus said, "He that is greatest among you, let him be your servant." With this he established the servant rather than the ruler image. A personal goal that will serve both God and mankind within the normal capacities of the individual and give some reasonable satisfaction for the contribution, makes every single soul needed, wanted, respected and even loved by those who know enough to really care. What more is there?

Finally, Jesus placed personal goals in their proper perspective when he so graciously corrected the evaluations of a good woman mentioned in Luke 11:27-28. As she heard the precious words fall from His lips, it seems that with a mother's love and pride she uttered "Blessed is the womb that bare thee, and the paps which thou hast sucked." Which the writer interprets as though she meant "What a joy to have been the mother of a young man like you!" To which Jesus replied, "Yea, *rather* blessed are they that hear the word of God and keep it!" With these words he forever swept away any special significance which this good woman sought to attach to "physically bringing him into the world." His reply seems to indicate "Woman, a *greater* personal goal and accomplishment is to *accept me* rather than just bear me!" In this way womanhood would be continually giving birth to both He and His cause. In this manner, any Christian woman on earth can call *"The Son—her Son!"*

Preacher, one of the goals of both good psychotherapy and preaching should be that of causing precious humble souls to feel they amount to something. That if they are in tune with God—*they are in turn tuning the world!*

202